# CREATIVE SOCIAL MINISTRY FOR THE CHURCH

*A plan for
week-day ministry
integrating social work methods
with a Biblical dynamic*

## Alpha Walters M. Melton
### Southwestern Baptist Theological Seminary

## BROADMAN PRESS
### Nashville, Tennessee

Deep gratitude is expressed to the publishers which have given

permission to use their copyrighted material shown in the footnotes

and Bibliography of this book and as shown below:

Campus Publishers, Ann Arbor, Michigan: Robert D. Vinter, Readings in
    Group Work Practice, 1968, pp. 20-27, 30-31.

Division of Missions, Home Mission Board, Southern Baptist Convention,
    Atlanta, Georgia: Jewell Beall, Baptist Centers Reaching a Con-
    temporary World, 1964, p. 17.

Harper and Row Publishers, Inc., New York, N.Y.: Sherwood Eliot Wirt,
    The Social Conscience of the Evangelical, 1968, p. 1.

J. B. Lippincott Company, Philadelphia, Pennsylvania: George D.
    Younger, The Church and Urban Renewal, pp. 126, 175, 191.

Moody Press, Moody Bible Institute of Chicago: Marion Nelson, Why
    Christians Crack Up, 1960, revised 1967, pp. 23-24.

Prentice-Hall, Inc., Englewood Cliffs, N.J.: Gisela Konopka, Social
    Group Work: A Helping Process, copyright 1963. Reprinted by
    permission of Prentice-Hall, Inc., Englewood Cliffs, N.J., pp.
    23, 29, 131, 167-170.

All Scripture references are from the King James Version.

## TABLE OF CONTENTS

## Preface

I am indebted to my husband, co-workers, and students who have encouraged the writing of this book and to Dorothy Pulley, Blanche Mohn, and Norma Wynn for their skill in typing and proof reading the manuscript. I acknowledge with grateful appreciation Southwestern Baptist Theological Seminary, Fort Worth, Texas, the personnel of the Southern Baptist Home Mission Board, Texas Baptists, and especially Joe Davis Heacock, Dean of the School of Religious Education, Southwestern Seminary, J. M. Price, Dean Emeritus, and Ellis L. Carnett, former pastor and Director of Texas Baptist Benevolences.

This book is not considered a scholarly product. Its purpose is to help students who are interested in church social work. It is also hoped that it may serve as a guide for churches in developing seven-day-a-week social ministries to meet the needs of people.

It is written in understandable, non-technical language for students, lay members of churches, and for staff and board members who desire to know more of the group work process in helping persons in trouble.

This book may add to the study, thought, prayer, and creative work in carrying out the responsibility of concern for those outside the church. A dream of more than twenty years is coming true as God opens the hearts of men and the doors of churches for the extension of compassionate services beyond the church members. There is no apology for the idea of integrating social work methods with biblical content. All Christians have a commitment to Jesus Christ as Saviour and Lord and to the Bible as their guide to faith and actions.

There is a scarcity of social work material written for the church. This book is designed to be used in training church leaders for more effective work with small groups. The chapter on creative ideas can be a guide for discussion groups for youth and adult classes in planning for the church outreach ministry or for solving existing social problems.

As Solomon stated that there is nothing new under the sun, I can say that there is nothing new related in this book. Every idea has been received from someone with whom I have had contact, from literature, or from the reigning, Loving Lord whom I love and serve.

Alpha W. Melton

Fort Worth, Texas

# CHAPTER I

## CHURCHES SCIENTIFICALLY PLAN
## FOR MINISTRIES

### Churches Desiring to Help

Churches of today are facing tremendous problems.
Many churches are discovering that a large number of their
members are driving from ten to fifteen miles on Sunday
to attend the services.  The community around the church
has new people who do not attend the church.  Some neighborhoods have more retired people and very few children.
The large one-family homes of the past are now housing
several families.  The traditional community has changed
so that the conventional church program seems to have little
attraction to the new neighbors.  There are suspicious and
fearful Negroes and whites, militants, forgotten children,
restless teenagers, lonely aging.  There is hopelessness,
discouragement, unemployment, and much need for medical
attention.

The church may need to be a voice for those whose
voices are so small or weak that they are not heard.  The
church is a part of the neighborhood, a religious and
social institution in the community with responsibility to
the people and to God for decisions and actions.  The Christ

1

who became flesh and showed Christians how to love and how to live is continually speaking to the church today. The church can minister to people as it speaks up and fights evil which hurts and hinders them, and can positively seek to destroy the breeding places of social evils. "The minister of a local congregation is a generalist who must concern himself with anything and everything that affects the life of his flock."[1] There is nothing wrong with using scientific methods so long as the church remains true to its main function. Many churches are being compelled to become involved in the community.

The church may be a true church of the Lord Jesus Christ or it may become like a large club. The ideas cited here can help to define which of the two the church really is

| A Club | The Church of Jesus Christ |
|---|---|
| 1. Exists for its members. | 1. Exists to win and save all mankind. |
| 2. Limits membership to those "like us." | 2. Accepts all who believe in Christ as members and opens its services to all. |
| 3. Plans programs to please and serve the interests of its members | 3. Plans programs to inspire and instruct its members by reaching out for new members by serving their needs. |
| 4. Moves with its members | 4. Seeks to serve all in its area. If the members move, they form or join other churches where they are. |

---

[1]George D. Younger, The Church and Urban Renewal (New York: J. B. Lippincott Company, 1965), p. 175.

2

| 5. | Resists changes that threaten the self-interests of its members. | 5. | Adapts to change with un-changeing love and purpose to serve. |
|---|---|---|---|
| 6. | Fights to preserve its budget and status. | 6. | Believes that in "losing" its life in service it will "find" its true life. It may need some help from more prosperous branches. |
| 7. | Does most of its work by paid staff in the club house. | 7. | Enlists its members in concern for and service to the whole world. |
| 8. | Often gives its members the feeling that "We're doing a great job; we're a big success." | 8. | Can never expect its members to feel that they are accomplishing the whole task, but does give them a deep sense of oneness with Christ and with one another.[1] |

Since government and city planners set the stage for conservation, redevelopment, or rehabilitation, the church wants to become involved, so as to influence social change. The church may not desire to adapt its program to deal with results of the policies. It may be that the influence of the church can be greater if it concerns itself with questioning the policies while they are being formed--the values, the benefits, the reality of whose interest is played up or helped, and many other ethical concerns.

It is not enough for churches and/or denominations to raise the above questions only when their church facilities or members are to be involved in the renewal plan. The church to be Christian is concerned about human beings and

---

[1] Ibid., p. 191.

how they are valued by their Creator.  If God cares, the Christian church also should care.  God has set men on earth to act and speak for Him in love and reconciliation.  He depends upon human instruments to do His work.

> Often the church is surrounded by human beings who need its ministry, but it has members who have no line of communication with the neighborhood people and no developed skills for meeting their needs.[1]

Some churches are employing a Christian social worker who helps bridge this gap to bring the church to the people. Many are concerned about the needs of the community and are desiring to creatively and redemptively participate in ministering to those within the reach of the church.  This ministry calls for dedicated hearts, hands, feet, and all that one is and has.

Many years ago the author was brought face-to-face with the fact of needing dedicated hands as well as heart. We were working in a community blighted with neglected children who felt hopeless and discouraged.  It was a few days before summer camp.  Some of the children were reported to have lice in their hair.  We knew if we went to camp with some having lice that before camp was over probably all of us would have lice.  What were we to do?  This was a new experience.  My husband went to a druggist to get something

---

[1] Jewel Chancy Beall, Baptist Centers Reaching a Contemporary World, Division of Missions, Home Mission Board (Atlanta, Georgia:  Southern Baptist Convention, 1964), p. 17.

to kill the lice and the mites. The "inspected" children
were sent to me--twenty-five at one time. I had a new, but
rewarding experience as I cautiously treated the scalps of
the children by applying "bornate." All of the children
could go to camp and none had to suffer from the lice
sucking their very life out of them. Heart concern wasn't
enough. Hands were compelled to work for God and others.
Often I called my doctor, the late J. H. Steger, or a
lawyer for advice. Then I would be able to minister with
knowledge gained just by asking. The use of community resources to meet human need can be both practical and effective. No one can know or do everything. The world problems
keep growing in spite of all that the church and other
agencies are doing. Churches are showing concern and desire to reach out to the lonely neighborhood through
various programs and services using the educational facilities of the church for the ministry seven days a week.
Volunteers are finding avenues whereby their training and
skill can be effectively used. Some have the greatest gift
of all--abounding love to share with those who have experienced little love.

### Advantages of the "New" Ministry

1.  Economical because the church facilities are
    used;
2.  Offers mission action opportunities for the
    entire church membership;

3. Provides an outreach to the community to help suffering humanity and lead them to the merciful Saviour;

4. Provides chances for working cooperatively with social and civic groups for community betterment;

5. Offers an outlet for professionals in the church to render unselfish service in the name of Christ;

6. Bridges the gap between classes and cultures and brings about unity in Christ;

7. Builds up feelings of being needed and useful among church members as well as among those outside the church;

8. Produces an atmosphere which is conducive to fuller commitment to Christ;

9. Makes the Church with Christ's message a living, vital, relevant reality;

10. Provides opportunity for creativity in a program that enhances and integrates the total church ministry;

11. Has drawing power to reach those who are in the "world";

12. Stimulates community change in social and moral standards;

13. Helps the church fulfil its mission of provision for worship, proclamation, healing, education and ministry;

6

14. Enhances spiritual development of Christians through personal involvement;

15. Shows Christian love through its concern and action of meeting human needs.

The late Rev. G. W. Burton, a beloved Negro pastor of Zion Baptist Church, Fort Worth, Texas, for over forty years loved the children of his neighborhood. For ten years I directed graded clubs in this church. If he could speak today to give the advantages of this outreach of love, he would tell of the boys who are now preaching the Gospel, or of the Sunday School teachers and other leaders who first came to Zion Church through week-day ministries. Often he would refer to the worth of the children being far greater than the building in which they left their foot prints on the floor or carpet.

Another who participated in another week-day ministry often spoke, saying, "I had a hard life. My husband drank and we never knew what it meant to have such friends as we have found in this place." This family was discovered in a house sleeping on newspapers on the floor. The church cared for this family. Food, clothing, furniture and a job for the father gave them a lift. The children were enrolled in kindergarten and the mother attended a sewing class. Family night at the church drew the entire family to become a part of the neighborhood, to see films, use thier talents, and

have fun with other families.  They found within the fellowship a greater love than that of mere human personalities.

## Principles as Guidelines

The principles outlined in this chapter may serve
as guidelines for any of the ministries suggested in Chapter
I--community center (Good Will Center), mission center, or
church week-day ministry.  Any type of service developed
should emerge out of concern for people in need.  Inves-
tigation of community need should proceed according to a
specific and scientific plan.  To avoid costly mistakes
extensive study and planning should be done before project-
ing a new program or service.  This calls for a professionally trained person and an efficient committee of community
leaders within the church.  The members should be responsible
persons who decide on a clear understanding of the kind of
information needed and who will only be satisfied with a
thorough study.  The procedure for the study should be
prayerfully and scientifically done.  The following ideas
may be helpful:

1.  Pray for God's Guidance

Prayer is necessary in any Christian endeavor.
The plan should be conceived, created and nurtured
in prayer.  This assures clear vision, guidance,
wisdom, and courage for the task, but it calls for
putting feet to the prayers to bring about--

2. Understand the Community

There are many community resources available
for gaining pertinent information for more awareness of people and their needs as well as to help
to recognize gaps in community services. The
following list gives some sources and the information which may be secured from each source. All
of these sources may not be in every neighborhood,
but some of them will be in all cities. The committee will determine which ones can be of help to
the church community study. Derrel Watkins, a
doctoral student in social work, Southwestern Baptist
Theological Seminary, Fort Worth, Texas, is presently
making a community survey, using the following resources, while a student in another school made a
survey of only the social agencies within the community to determine the gaps in service and how the
church could become a serving church.

| Resource | Information |
|---|---|
| Government Census Reports | Statistics on population such as race, nationality, the number and size of families, age groupings, employment figures with the number of workers in each local industry the range of wages. |
| Housing Commission | Housing conditions. |
| Planning firms, Zoning Board and Chamber of Commerce | Plans for housing, industrial centers, etc. |

| | |
|---|---|
| Health Department | Health conditions, needs and facilities. |
| Welfare Department | Intensity of welfare needs, those receiving public assistance, gaps in service. |
| Board of Education | School enrollment, truancy, etc. |
| Juvenile Court | Statistics on crime and delinquency. |
| Police Department | Problem areas, crimes, etc. |
| Recreation Department | Available resources in the community. |
| City Library | Location of libraries, book mobile services and needs. |
| Churches and association | Names and location of churches and missions. |
| Historical Societies | Religious background of the people. |
| Social services | Community characteristics, needs, trends, social agencies and institutions. |
| House-to-house Survey | Effective for discovering family and community needs. |
| Church Records | Information about members, budgets, mobility of members |
| Public Utility Companies | Telephone numbers, type of fuel and water supply. |
| Local political parties | Up to date community profile. |
| Highway Department | Maps and plans for new highways. |

When facts are gathered from any or all of these sources, community life and need may be more easily determined. Recommendations for the program or services if made to meet needs will make the Christian gospel relevant to those whom the conventional church program has made no appeal.

3. Securing Interest and Responsible Involvement of the Church

A church that is to sponsor creative social work ministries must be cognizant of what is involved in such a ministry. After prayer, a report is then given by the "Study and Survey Committee" to the entire church in business session. A challenging address on meeting the needs should stir the church to action. A motion should be made to establish a program to meet the needs revealed in the report. After the vote and acceptance of this motion, another motion should be made to organize an Advisory Board or Committee of Social Ministries. It has proved helpful to have this committee composed of representatives from each church organization with some members at large. The latter group might include a teacher, lawyer, doctor, builder, and others who can give wise counsel. One church which is beginning to develop a weekday ministry has the regular mission committee of the church to serve with the weekday director as the advisory group. Each church will develop its own plan of procedure. A designated time for the first Board (or Committee) meeting should be set and an appeal made for volunteers who will indicate the type of service they ca render.

At the first meeting the committee should organize, select a chairman, secretary, and other necessary officers. Simple by-laws to guide the program or service may be adopted indicating the name of the program, function, membership, officers committees, time and place of meeting, personnel, etc. There should be appointment of necessary committees such as Personnel, Program, Transportation, Finance, and others the committee deems necessary. Plans should be made for employment of a full-time, professionally trained Director for the week-day program. A person with a Master of Religious Education and a Master of Social Work degree will best best equipped for such a task. Sometimes a lay person within the church is trained to direct the work

At a second meeting of the Board the Finance Committee should present the budget for consideration and adoption. The budget should be included in the general church budget and should include the salary of a director, other staff, utilities, supplies for the clubs, services, and classes, janitorial help, etc. The name of the director should be presented to the church for approval. The selectio

of carefully chosen volunteers for leaders and
workers for various activities and age groups
should be done after the director is on the field.
A schedule for the beginning of the ministry may
be adopted at this meeting. No one schedule can
be used. The needs of the people, the availability
of a meeting place, and the time suitable to workers
will determine the schedule.

## Train Volunteers

After the Church and its Board have made the necessary preparation the director begins a program for training
of volunteers. This may include personal conferences with
group leaders, classes, films, observations or internships
in churches having such a ministry, workshops, seminars,
field trips, and appropriate reading materials.

An effective week-day social ministries director
who has the responsibility for leadership training must
know what the broad purposes and goals are as well as have
skill to help each staff member to develop responsibly in
patterns of work and in methods. It is also necessary for
him to provide an atmosphere which is conducive to effectiveness.

The executive charged with leadership training holds
the key to his and to the other staff members' success.
This is true in his conception of himself and of the esteem
he has of persons and their ability to accomplish a creative

13

job as they work together.  Some factors necessary for
effective directors are:

1.  Be convinced that the work is necessary.

2.  Enlist the ideas and skills of the workers
in goal-setting.

3.  Encourage workers to make their own plans of
procedure.

4.  Be available for conferences when needed.

5.  Have confidence in and trust staff members
to do their jobs.

6.  Be approachable, enthusiastic, and supportive.

7.  Be an encourager to motivate staff members to
strive for the best in doing their partnership
task.

Other important factors are:

Promotions, increase in salary, and fringe benefits
promote better job performance.

Promote expression of both positive and negative
feelings.

Organization, general supervision, continuous planning, and evaluations of the program.

Working with staff and community agencies.

Working with committees or Board:  giving reports,
managing finances, and other business.

Speaking concerning the work and needs.

14

Continuous integrating of new members brought into the church through the week-day ministry.

After workers are trained and each has definite understandings of jobs (job descriptions), the program and services should be well advertised and started. Workers should continually follow up the meetings with home visits by group members. Staff meetings, conferences, and on-the-spot evaluations should be regularly held for improvement and adaptation where needed.

The duties of the director and the staff should be adequately specified. All of them work closely with the pastor and other church staff members. Relationships are very important; in fact, they can hardly be exaggerated. It is the soul of the ministry. It is a life-giving principle which makes the entire ministry a warm, humane, and effective helping experience. Good relationship is "contagious"--it is felt but can hardly be understood apart from experience. Intellectual understanding of relationship certainly does not always give skill in using it. It often becomes hard work to practice it.

## Effective Programming

There is not a set plan for program. Each situation is different and unique, calling for a program designed to meet particular needs. The program should be person-entered and involve the members in planning with the workers' help. The findings in the specific community study

should designate the type of program to be projected. One
church started recreation, day care, and graded clubs, drama
and music groups, and family night programs. Another might
start a drop-in center for the lonely aging persons. A
tutoring and literacy program, classes of various kinds, and
clinics if there are none in the community. It might be
felt that satellite fellowships or Bible Clubs in selected
homes in various city blocks would help the shy, frightened
neighborhood to know the concern and compassion of the
church. One church discovered a need for friends and fellow
ship for internationals. The group worker is to help the
group members to develop a program rather than "put on" or
"put over" some cut-and-dried plan; however, the worker may
need much resource material and ideas from which choices can
be made.

There is no limit to the possibilities for growth
for inner-city church programs and services. The program wi
be continuously changing and expanding as the spirit of love
and friendly helpfulness gets to be known throughout the com
munity. A week-day program started by the writer included a
kindergarten and a system of graded clubs. Soon a day care
program was added which led to the beginning of a medical
clinic. The clinic revealed great need for nutrition and
prenatal classes. The director should be alert to changes
and needs and promote creativity in program development.
Expansion of program requires enlargement of staff and

16

larger and better facilities. Presently, one church needs fifteen extra rooms to house the large number of children enrolled, while another church needs a large building which is appropriate for recreational activities.

The procedure for programming will be governed by community needs, skills of the staff, building facilities, schedule, etc. It seems best to start with a few activities, make the program interesting and challenging, and do not be afraid to try something "brand new." The Bible and its principles should be the center of a church program. The author has been interested in reading and observing Christians in many helping professions who are boldly synthesizing and correlating Christian theology into their professional practice outside the church building. My own concept goes along with these in the field of social work, psychiatry, and psychology for the Church is wherever the true Christian is. Since God has dominion over and regulates His universe, including human beings, the author could not dare ignore God and His power to work in and through persons. The author feels that wherever possible the church should work with community agencies to meet many of the needs discussed here, lest the church get involved with many good things and neglect the main task of the church. No one church can provide all of the needed services or program. It can be aware of community resources and work cooperatively with them to more completely meet all of the needs within the neighborhood.

17

From more than twenty years of experience in week-day work it seems that the program of a church might be built around the many requests for help which point up real community needs. Some guidelines are suggested from calls which came directly to my husband and me or through some other staff or group member. All of the program suggestions were not developed in our work, but have been effective in some churches of various denominations with which the author is familiar.

1. Health and Welfare

Clinics meeting weekly with volunteer doctors and nurses within the church membership or from the community. Some clinics are done in cooperation with the local Health Department.

Pediatric

General-examinations of children and others.

Dental--local dentists sometimes donate a half-day of service.

Maternal or well-baby clinic in cooperation with local health department.

Eye, ear, nose and throat.

Mental health--psychiatric clinic in cooperation with community hospital or agency.

Health education--this may be done in cooperation with Health Department, local home economists, and other professional persons.

First aid and home nursing--the Red Cross will cooperate in this program
Planned parenthood done in cooperation with a local
agency
Nutrition classes, meal planning and serving--local
home economics teachers or home demonstration
workers are usually glad to help
Loan fund to help maintain self-respect and pre-
vent dependency
Buyers club of a small number of families to help
each other buy wisely and save money
Emergency gifts--food, clothing, medicine, etc.
Referrals--family services, foster homes, vocational training and rehabilitation, etc.
Legal aid--contacts with courts, welfare department,
juvenile detention workers, and others
Counseling with persons with all types of problems
Patterning exercises for brain damaged (discussed
in Chapter IV)
2. Employment
Some centers have employment bureaus
Referral services to free public employment offices
and/or to private agencies
Church members help in vocational and on-the-job
training--mechanic, carpentry, appliance repair,
plumbing, electrical work, maid training, laundry and home services (yard work, washing

windows, house cleaning)

Telephone system where a number is given for emergency cases for job recommendations

3. Educational-Recreational

Library, reading room and study hall

Guidance, tutoring, literacy classes for adults by local qualified persons

Referrals to public schools, night schools, trade schools, schools for exceptional children, scholarship possibilities

Cooperation with visiting teachers, school counselors and social workers

Classes of whatever type is needed--prenatal, nutrition, English

Special-interest centers and groups--budgeting, sewing, cooking, hat-making, flower arrangement

Music--listening to good music, participating in Musical groups--vocal, choruses, choirs, sing-in, etc. Instrumental groups--bands, orchestras, stringed quartets, bell ringers, rhythm band, kitchen band, or individual instruction

Drama--acting in a play, choral reading, creating experience and producing pageants and such like

Social--parties, banquets, picnics, teas, receptions, etc.

Gameroom, gymnasium, playground

Day camps, retreats, week-end camps, family camps.

Barber shops, beauty parlors, and grooming classes.

A graded system of Bible clubs for each age group.

Kindergarten

Day care, one-day or one-half day care for free
time for mothers, night care, and nursery
school, story hours (doll club, play house),
day care for aged who need this help.

Discussion groups

Street and/or block clubs

Arts, crafts, sports, athletics, photography.

Trips to places of interest - libraries, schools,
churches, museums, zoos, airports, indust-
ries, social agencies.

4. Youth and Family Services

Counseling services

Juvenile rehabilitation

Guidance to children and parents

Big-brother and big-sister plan

Referrals when problem is deep seated

Utilization of skills of psychiatrist and
social workers in the church membership

Foster home care when needed

Marital difficulties

Legal aid

Consumer education

Utilization of lawyers in the church member-
ship to offer free week-end service
Child placement
Work collaboratively with licensed child
placing agencies, children's homes, etc.
Spiritual help
Man-boy matching when boys need help
Big-sister plan where girls need help
Families matched together for socialization,
spiritual development, or other needs
Bible study and prayer groups
5. Religious Training
Graded Bible study presented to meet all age
levels.
Develop witnesses to win the lost to Christ.
Provide an atmosphere of love and acceptance.
Small prayer groups
Area home fellowships where guidance pro-
motes spiritual development

Commitment to Christ involves more than the suggestions of this chapter. The true Christian church must
really care enough to share and become involved with neighbors and the "small" world, making Christ and His wonderful
love known through a compassionate and evangelical social
thrust. "A Christian literacy team, on safari deep in the
Congo, devotes weeks to the task of teaching primitive

22

Africans to read and write. To the tribespeople the members of the team say, 'We learned this from Jesus"'.[1] The church to really be the church must _be_ like Jesus. The greatest impressions are made when broken humanity sees the church busy "being" a servant to those needing its ministry.

Through the services and the program both the church members and those outside the membership will have been helped. Through experiences many people have found not only social and material help but have found an abiding faith for spiritual enrichment and have become a part of the church fellowship.

"The church's mission carries it out into the world around it. Only when God's seeking love is brought to unreconciled humanity can the miracle of redemption transform the life of the world."[2] The ministry of the church must involve witnessing as service is offered. The church must be careful to continually evaluate its mission and ministry, lest it only become a humanitarian outreach of good works 'indistinguishable from secular community agencies."[3]

---

[1]Sherwood Eliot Wirt, The Social Conscience of the Evangelical (New York: Harper and Row, 1968), p. 1.

[2]Younger, The Church and Urban Renewal, p. 125.

[3]Ibid., p. 126.

23

# CHAPTER II

## GROUP WORK THE MOST EFFECTIVE METHOD

### What Is a Group?

A group is not just a cluster or number of people meeting together. The observing worker can soon tell when a group is forming by what the members say with reference to others or how they feel about others in the group. If members speak of "our" club or "my" club and there is a feeling of "ours" or "we-ness," then the worker can feel that a group is forming. There is a friendly, cooperative team spirit. It is not uncommon for the membership ties of a group to become so strong that they will take up for each other, endure pain for the group, or defend each other against criticism from outside persons. There is a quality of pride, commitment, and togetherness which brings cohesiveness.

A group may have cohesiveness which binds members together, yet may be unable to be productive or have the ability to work together effectively. Some groups may be low in their cohesiveness but high in productivity. The author worked for several months with a small group of

entally retarded teenagers. After several meetings there
as a bond between the girls. Friendship ties were formed.
hey liked to be together and showed a great deal of pride
n belonging to the club. At first they were unable to be
roductive in taking responsible jobs; however, toward the
nd of the sixth month, they became more skillful in working
uccessfully together. They shared the same norms and were
o attracted to the group that some showed resistance to
eaving the group when they were moved from one building to
nother. They were motivated to participate as a group and
t was felt that before eight months had passed that there
as coordination of the group efforts by the members of the
lub.

## What Is Group Work?

There are many definitions of group work. "The
onception of social work should be kept fluid in order to
aintain in this profession at least an open mind toward
umanity's changing needs and the best methods for meeting
hem."[1] This same concept is held by many for the method
f group work. Some people think of recreation as social
roup work. Recreation may be one tool or technique used
n group work to meet certain needs, but there are numer-
us other tools used to meet individual needs such as:
afts, discussion, role playing, field trips, education,

[1]Gisela Konopka, Social Group Work: A Helping
rocess (Englewood Cliffs, N. J.: Prentice-Hall, Inc.,
963), p. 23.

25

creative arts, and many others.

Group work is one of three primary methods used to fulfill social work functions. The others are case work and community organization. Secondary methods are administration, research, teaching or education. Group therapy aims at relieving suffering through protected and controlled group interaction with the help of a professional worker. Social group work is thought of as "helping" a group or of "treating" a group, signifying that healthy or sick individuals are helped through groups. Social group work "helps individuals to enhance social functioning through purposeful group experiences and to cope more effectively with their personal, group or community problems."[1]

It is a planned way of working with people in groups. It is an orderly way of conducting different activities for the development of persons. Individuals in groups experience growth through guided group interaction. The worker never loses sight of the individual in the group but uses the group to help each individual.

## Group Composition and Size

Church groups are formed in various ways by different denominations. Most churches receive all persons into groups in a week-day program if they first sign a form or

_____

[1]Ibid., p. 29.

register, thus, declaring interest and intention to attend a particular group. Some require attendance of two or three meetings of a particular group each week as prerequisites to membership. Others may have a small club membership fee to help pay for certain materials.

Group composition varies with the aims and purposes of the group, the problems to be solved, and the characteristics of the group members. More than twenty years of experience working with groups has brought some very strong convictions to the writer. Chronological age and sex are not the only criteria for forming groups. Joe was a large twelve-year-old in his age group. His behavior stuck out like a sore thumb. There was real danger that the other boys would take on his "bad" behavior. The rest of the group members were well matched, felt comfortable and congenial and could enjoy and participate in a number of common interests together. Joe was moved to a group just older than he, but where his size did not "show" up. He soon fit into the group and began to have opportunities for "prestige" in this group. Group composition can become a problem unless "trouble" factors are taken into consideration.

If normal children are placed with a group which has extremely bad and unacceptable behavior, the normal may act like the tough ones. The result is likely to be conflict between the members leading to anxiety. A beautiful, unwanted, normal girl was placed with a group of mental retardates who had had little if any socialization. Before

27

long her behavior was the same as that of the retardates.
Grouping may be a serious threat to group members, however,
it may not always produce trouble if there is a skillful
worker.

Often we have found that those who cause the most
trouble are the ones who need the group experience the most.
Some experiences which have helped if groups were too large
or were not matched for the greatest growth and development
are:

1. Form sub-groups within the larger group.

2. Offer a variety of choices in program activities.

3. Have flexibility of program.

4. Provide a special skilled worker.

5. Give individualized attention of group members
by worker inside and outside the group meeting
through home visits, or make special requests
for a "troubled" member to help the worker in
special tasks.

6. Change of programs to something very uncommon
and interesting.

The size of the group should vary according to purposes, age, rules, facilities, interests and abilities of
members, and the number of group workers. In one experience
the size of the group was limited to five members because
only five children and a driver could ride in the "State Car

This was a group of children in a State School for mentally retarded. One of the worker goals was providing social experiences for the retardates with "normal" peers outside the institution. In this case rules of the institution and goals determined the size of the group.

The typical size in most of the church club groups with which the writer is familiar is from twelve to twenty members from age nine up. They are usually made up of one sex and are of about the same age. If there are less than five to eight or more than twenty-five in one group it is difficult to develop or maintain a close bond or interest in an activity.

Small groups (interacting between two or more people) are better than larger groups if the goals are for "helping" or "treating" the members with some kind of problem, such as communication, socialization with peers, or for developing certain skills. Usually there is a closer bond of fellowship and a more therapeutic relationship in a small group. Large groups are effective when the purpose is to share information, share experiences, inspire or unify, entertain, listen to a lecture or sermon, gain support for a special project, or explore the idea of some specific plan. Large groups may be more formal or more structured than a small group. The small group is a little democracy which serves as a voice and a bridge from the group to the larger society. Sometimes in large groups there may be an individual who experiences "healing" as he becomes aware of a

29

personal need through listening or looking. His needs are met as he identifies with a message and the messenger. Sue was a teenager experiencing many bodily changes. She felt that she was "different" from others her age. As she listened to a school nurse explain the growing-up process, she was relieved of her feeling of differentness. Sally, a divorcee, felt that she had committed the unpardonable sin. She was helped through a sermon in her church which explained God's love and mercy of forgiveness for sin.

## Group Work Principles

The principles or ideas of individuals who make up groups came from the Creator. They have been emphasized in the Bible, by scientists and are basic to all practice of social work. It has been interesting to observe students in classes as they searched the Scripture and found examples of social work principles. The worker must understand not only the ideas but also the forces and influences back of the principles. Changing times have brought new techniques and challenges in group work. These ideas apply to small as well as to large groups.

1. Behavior is contagious and the right kind of groups can have healing power. To be a positive potential for individual as well as group growth there should be careful planning in forming groups.

2. Every church group should be developed and carried out with specific goals and purposes. The church, group worker, group, and individuals will have goals. All of these should meet the needs of persons within the different groups. The informality of small groups does not give way to an undisciplined, haphazardly done job. There must be real purpose planned and carried out.

3. Genuine acceptance of persons as individuals of dignity and worth, yet recognizing strengths and weaknesses, has great power. The relationship is a two-way acceptance, as the worker accepts individuals, they in turn accept the worker. This relationship becomes a major technique for individual and group growth.

4. The worker's confidence in persons stimulates them to change and develop. Because individuals and groups are uniquely different and are continually changing and developing, the worker must continually give attention to the individual needs of each member, as well as of each group. Jesus never lost sight of an individual. A good group worker in a church will want to follow this example.

5. The group worker is similar to a coach of a team in that he carefully guides the

31

interactions between members and encourages and
enables each member to behave in such a way
that the entire group will be benefited. This
interaction energy is the soul of group work
and is a powerful influence which stimulates
change. People respond to those who notice and
accept them. The worker guides in order to re-
lease as well as to increase or limit member
interaction. He is not to tell the group but
lead them to assume responsibility and work out
plans through participation of one with another

6. According to the capacity of the group members
the worker stimulates group planning and decision-making. Members develop and assume
responsibility  by being confronted with the
chance, as well as the responsibility, to act
democratically as the group determines its goal
and procedures. Experiences, competencies, and
skills are tested, tried, and developed as the
group itself assumes direction. Self direction
comes to the group gradually as the worker help
members to behave responsibly. Some members
may need special help, calling for the worker t
act in the role of executive, giving direction
and encouragement to greater capacity for responsible actions. The group develops in togetherness with members as well as with the wo

7. As the group changes and develops the organization changes. There must be flexibility in organization and program. There needs to be enough formal organization to channel the energies of group members in the right direction. Orderliness gives certainty and security to the members and opens up opportunities for the group to choose its leaders to get the jobs done. The group is free to organize itself and work out plans and processes, the number and type of officers, group goals, program, etc. The worker must help the group to recognize and set out the qualifications for leaders. The leaders must then be oriented into what is expected in the different responsible jobs. The worker enables officers to be successful in the various roles, without taking away from them or taking over.

8. The program begins with need, interest, and capacity of the group and then should provide continuous and progressive experience. The beginning may seem very small, but it starts right where the group is. It enlarges as ideas, suggestions, and interests broaden.

9. The group uses the wider environment with its many resources to enrich the program and broaden

the experiences of the individual members. The
use of community resources is educational and
can have great influence upon group members. Th
developing group can also influence the community and its affairs.

10. The program, process, and results are con-
stantly evaluated. The worker influences the
group along with the church to look back to
see what has been accomplished. How has the
group attained its goals? How well has the
group met the needs and desires of its members?
Where have we succeeded, or failed?

Konopka discusses fourteen principles, eight of whic
are included here:

1. Appropriate modification of the group process
to help bring about desired change (such as strengthen
the isolate and help him to become a part of the group)
2. Encouragement of each member to participate
according to the stage of his capacity, enabling him to
become more capable.
3. Enabling members to involve themselves in the
process of problem solving.
4. Enabling group members to experience increasing
satisfactory forms of working through conflicts.
5. Provision for opportunities for new and differi
experiences in relationships and accomplishments.
6. Judicious use of limitations related to the dia
nostic assessment of each individual and the total situ
ation.
7. Purposeful and differential use of program
according to diagnostic evaluation of individual member
group purpose, and appropriate social goals.
8. Warm, human, and disciplined use of self on the
part of the group worker.[1]

---

[1]Konopka, Social Group Work: A Helping Process, pp
167-170.

## The Use of Democracy

The American democratic ideal is carried on in small groups. Many persons grew up in a family where it was important to cooperate with other members of the family. If one grows up to love and respect the other family members and the group enjoys doing things for each other, as well as doing things together as a family, this would be a democratic family.

One family consisting of the parents, two sons, and one daughter exemplified democracy in a difficult situation. The father was away from home in the service of his country. The mother and children had some difficult times at home. On one occasion the family council met to discuss a financial problem. One of the boys needed a new suit and the daughter needed a new coat. There was only enough money to buy one. The discussion was open. Upon realizing the situation, the daughter suggested that since the mother was a good seamstress that maybe she could make the coat and buy the suit. This was agreed upon in a very democratic manner and all of the family needs were met.

When a child starts to school he broadens his circle of friends. The public school is a result of groups working together. The church likewise is a cooperative fellowship. The social agencies in the community are products of cooperative effort. The government and laws reveal combined

effort. The city calls for group planning. The lighted
houses and streets shine forth to remind the public that all
things are done for people.

The child makes new friends away from home. Many
remain friends from grade school throughout life. They
play together and learn much from each other. There is
enjoyment in play and then in work. Persons can develop
in self expression, understanding, solving problems, changing
attitudes and behavior as they meet and participate in life
situations with other people.

The democratic society is a goal to provide for the
attainment of the highest potential of each individual and
provide the opportunity for him to stand in his place as a
responsible member of the society of people. The roots of
democracy lie in experience, behavior, and in Christian
ideals. The roots must grow deep into the human personality
lest they be uprooted by external or even internal enemies.
The democratic society was founded on faith in God. The
church has a profound responsibility in this crucial time
to help get the roots of democracy way down deep into the
personalities of the children and youth. The Nation of
America will be democratic as are the neighborhoods and com-
munities. Church group work has a tremendous challenge in
every neighborhood.

Growing leaders through participation in groups can
begin with little children. Children like to share and

36

assume responsibility for their group. Through experiences they can learn to get along with and relate to many different persons. The school age child and some pre-schoolers like to be a proud voice for their groups, and become helpers. Children can very early develop responsibility so as to be counted upon to do jobs they agree to do. The church can plan for its community so that its entire neighborhood will strengthen democracy. Small groups are more effective than large groups in developing the democratic process or in maintaining a democratic climate because of the opportunities for group decision-making. Each individual in a small group can have freedom for expression as well as feeling a part of the collective actions of the group.

## The Worker with a Group

The term worker is chosen rather than leader because of several reasons: (1) there are times when the worker refrains from leading the group; (2) the group experiences are to develop leaders within the group; (3) there are many other roles for the worker besides leading; (4) the worker uses many different means for helping the group rather than leading; and (5) the term group worker implies that the person has knowledge and skill and is a qualified, mature person. The group worker may be professionally trained to help individuals in groups develop goals, programs, process, etc. for themselves. The worker enables the group to be self-directing as they assume responsibility to carry out their plans. He begins with the group where the members are in their development and expects them to make progress at their own pace, according to their ability.

The desire of the worker is to help individuals in the group to develop and maintain satisfying, constructive, and productive relationships. Group members are helped to get along together and cooperate in various ways for the good of the group. This calls for a positive relationship between the worker and the group.

(1) The Group Itself

The group may be a _natural_ group - persons of the same sex, age, neighborhood, and of common interests. These similarities combine to create a close bond of congeniality, which is basic for forming a self-determining, self-governing club. Another type of group is the _artificial_ group which is brought together by an adult worker. It may be formed on the basis of age, sex, etc., as the natural group. This makes it possible for those who might not be chosen by peers to become a part of a group. The church groups more often are of the artificial type of formation because it is the desire of Christian workers that every person be included:

> We see the general sequence of the group work process as moving from "getting to know each other" (and in the hostile person this includes much trying out of the person he considers responsible or in authority) to deep affection (and sometimes dependency and jealousy of the sharing with other members) to the working through of one's problems or handicaps on a verbal

38

or non-verbal level to renewed trying out (but on a
level different from in the beginning) to a moving
out to healthy and normal relationships with adults
and children and the need for and the beginning to
actively reach out for achievement.[1]

(2)  Ways of Helping

The two ways of helping are direct and indirect.
Vinter lists four direct ways of influencing persons and
six means of using indirect influences.  These are listed
and discussed below.

A.  Direct Influence

a.  "Worker as central person - object of identification and drives"

The worker has a significant role in the group,
the position given to him by the church, and the
psychological influence he has upon the individual
members.  This pre-eminence may come from: initi-
ating the beginning of the group; the role and the
authority vested in him by the church; the knowledge
and skill which he has and uses in making available
to the group the resources and facilities of the
community which enhance his prestige; and the other
personal attributes regarding his personality, competencies, and skills.

b.  "Worker as symbol and spokesman - agent of
legitimate norms and values"

Many individuals served through groups mani-
fest various types of difficulties with regard to

---

[1]Konopka, _Social Group Work:  A Helping Process_,
p. 162.

the values and norms. These problems may stem from social functioning problems, from being members with deviants of sub-cultures, or from unacceptable social values they have internalized. Other group members may be reasonably free from such difficulties. One of the goals of group work usually is socialization, the acquisition of norms and values and behavioral standards acceptable by the larger society. The worker is the model to mediate these values, norms, appropriate roles, rules, laws, patterns of conduct, and attitudes.

The above modeling by the worker is seen in his behavior, outlook, what he does and does not participate in, the responses he makes, and through his attitudes and treatment of others. The worker must at times be a voice or spokesman to exemplify values and norms, set limits on behavior by requesting, requiring, or forbidding. He voices expectations regarding behavior by encouraging, rewarding, or punishing group members for their behavior. Rewards and punishments are usually material or social (e.g., praise). The worker may be required at times to use his powers of coercion and physically prevent one from assaulting another person, or may eject him from the group. It is usually best to use positive rather than negative techniques.

Rewards or inducements are better than depriva-
tions or punishments. Ejecting one from the
group should be a last resort.

c. "Worker as motivator and stimulator - definer
   of individual goals and tasks"

Workers often need to motivate members toward
specific goals or objectives by encouraging individual objectives, undertaking some specific
project, developing certain skills, or engaging
in new activities or some new interest. The
worker may introduce or employ incentives, inducements, or rewards to motivate members. The techniques of suggesting, proposing, encouraging, or
displaying enthusiasm are effective with some
individuals. The worker may need to personally
instruct individuals in some areas.

d. "Worker as executive - controller of membership roles"

The worker may assign tasks or projects or
divide the responsibilities for members according
to their abilities. He helps them to perform the
tasks, but does not do the task for any member.
He may directly work with an individual to de-
crease his deviant behavior. This may be done by
letting him know what the acceptable norms are, or
building up his self-esteem through rewards of
support, complimenting him for something he does

41

well, or the worker may set limits on how he can or cannot behave within the group. The worker is responsible for guiding interaction which is conducive to proper growth and development for each group member.

B. Indirect Influence

a. Goals and purposes

The worker goals set up for the group have a distinct influence upon the group members. The worker goals correspond to the church goals. A group may be chosen to fulfill some specific goals of the church and of the worker. Groups may have freedom to set their own goals, however the worker still has specific goals for the group. Sometimes very broad understandings are set up for a group and the group functions within these plans. Often the worker carefully redirects or modifies goals.

The goals have a powerful influence on members. Vinter gives these influences:

1. Selection of clients (members) for the group may be made explicitly with reference to its established purposes.
2. The individual client's (member's) attraction to and satisfaction with the group is partially dependent on its purposes.
3. The purposes of the group are also determinative of the distribution of leadership functions and member roles within it, thereby significantly affecting the experience of each client member.

4. . . . .group goals shape the program and
activity sequences developed in pursuit of these
ends.
5. . . . .group purposes will have some impli-
cation for the particular kind of decision-making
and governing procedures to be employed.[1]

Goals and purposes change from time to time

within a group.  The worker should keep in mind

the distinction between his aims and group pur-

poses to avoid the assumption that his goals have

been accepted by the group.

b.  Group Member Selection

In churches this becomes a problematic aspect

for the worker as well as for the group members.

The worker may not be able to select the members

for a group.  Often age and sex are the deter-

mining factors for group composition, which means

that there are differences in the kinds of interests,

capacities, and experiences.  Inter-personal re-

lations can become most difficult, as well as offer

few real satisfactions to members.  Composition

controls the capacity of the group to meet the

goals of the individual, group, and worker.

In churches there are children as well as youth

and adults who have social relationship problems

involving peers, parents, or others.  There should

be specific groups formed for members with different

[1]Robert D. Vinter, Readings In Group Work Practice
Ann Arbor, Mich.:  Campus Publishers, 1968), pp. 30-31.

problems so that programs, services, or activities
may be planned for specific needs. The group itself is a powerful force if it develops cohesiveness, mutuality, etc. This calls for similarity
of interests, capability, and experiences. Com-
patibility in groups depends upon the type of
group and its program, personality of individuals,
and capacity for different individuals to become
compatible.

c.  Group Size

The worker must know the individuals so that
he can determine the effects the size of the group
has upon the members. Research and experience
have shown that the larger group demands more in
leadership ability and less participation on the
part of members. Large groups can attempt tasks
which are impossible for small groups. Sub-groups
within a larger group can be effective.

Small groups permit more participation and
group decision-making. Interpersonal relations
among individuals tend to be greater. Members are
more likely to find status in a small group. The
worker has a greater opportunity to cope with behavior problems in a small group.

d.  Group procedures

Democratic procedures have been highly favored
because of the principle of self-determination or

self-direction. Guidance with permissiveness, warmth, friendliness, and helpfulness in contacts with individuals has been the characteristic role of group workers. The degree of self-government varies from group to group according to the type and purpose of the group and the age and ability of the members. Strict control by the worker leads to dependence upon the worker, and limits personal development of members as well as the satisfaction one derives from the group experience.

Rigid parliamentary procedures may stifle the group. Simple agreements that each person is as important as another and has a right to express himself, the majority is the basis for decision, sharing, and taking turns may be more effective than the rigid use of parliamentary rules. It is important that groups practice decision-making. This develops more personal member satisfactions.

This use of officers in a club is for the use of democratic process and to provide development roles for members. Often this is not the result. Formal structure does not necessarily guarantee the above desires. Patterns may need to be created to get the desires accomplished. It has proved very helpful by the writer to pass around the officerships, i.e., one serve as president one

time or for several meetings and then another take
his turn. This calls for extra guidance on the
part of the worker, but it may be beneficial to
the group. The age and capacity of group members
help determine the type of organization. Some
groups desire a formal organization.

e. Group development

Group workers are concerned with the development process. Their plan is to help members develop to their highest potential. Interaction between
worker-member and member-member largely influences
the rate and the direction of group movement. The
worker must know when and how to intervene, as well
as what stage of development to expect within the
group. Intervention by the worker demands that he
know the group, as well as recognize the meanings
of interaction and the potentials for change or
development of members. It is also important that
the worker be cognizant of the external influences
upon the group. If there are problems, consider
how they can be solved.

f. Programming

The worker should have knowledge of community
resources and of the range of services and activities available to meet the goals of the group. It
is important to plan for a progressive program

development for a specific period of time in accordance with the goals. Imbedding certain activities into the on-going process is essential to prevent having unrelated events inappropriate for the development process.

The choice of activities should be aimed toward goals, directed at meeting individual as well as group needs, be specific to capabilities of members, and be designed so that modifications may be used to enhance the most effective results.[1]

C. Dealing with Problems

Every group worker is guaranteed to have some problems. Solving problems is a sure way to provide growth experience for an individual and a group. Very little real growing occurs as long as everything runs smoothly. Problems are more easily handled if the worker and the group know what the problems are. Facing reality is rather difficult but it must be done if problems are to be solved.

An honest look at these problems reveal several important things for workers. Problems are created by persons -- often the leaders who have attempted using the wrong method or technique. Problems start as little ones but build up to large ones because people often think they will work out by themselves. The old adage that a "stitch in time saves

---

[1]Vinter, Readings In Group Work Practice, pp. 20-27.

47

nine" really works at this point. If workers are alert and work out problems as they arise, much time, energy, and hurt can be avoided. A lack of understanding of purposes and goals, or lack of or too much organization will result in problems. A cold impersonal organization breeds problems, whereas, a warm personal interest can help overcome problems. Expecting too much too soon of a group or having a round peg in a square hole are sure to bring trouble and lack of satisfaction. Worn-out ideas, tired individuals, and failure to be honest in the work and in being alert to do continuous evaluation are sure to create problems.

Every church should have a "skill bank", i.e., a file of church members giving special skills of each so that persons might be useful in the ministry. Often there are a few who do all the leadership roles, a few who do all the teaching and even the praying. There are in many large churches scores of untapped resources, many who need to feel really wanted and needed. For example, the retired persons often have many skills which should be put to work for the Lord through the church. There is one church, which has 5,000 in Sunday School, and has only the pastor, several secretaries, and one other professional worker.

In dealing with conflict it is recognized that the following factors help in group work.

1. Be open and realistic about problems.
2. Pinpoint the problem.
3. Deal with the problem rather than the person.
4. Help the persons involved to determine the
   points of disagreement and make plans to work
   it out.
5. When agreements have been made drop it and
   move on.

Problems are really individual behavioral problems,
interpersonal relationship problems, problems within a
group which may be related to leadership, relationships,
lack of understanding, wrong motives, or attitudes, or
problems with relationship between groups such as jealousy,
strife, rivalry, competition.

Workers learn how to become better workers through
education, experience, through solving problems and helping
groups solve problems. It makes no difference what problems
come to a worker, but it makes a great deal of difference
what he does with the problem. It is better for one to get
on top of a problem than to let the problem get on top of
the worker. Problems and conflicts are sure to come but
they can become the stuff from which comes progress and
victory. Those who have a living faith in the Lord know
that victory can be theirs with the help of the Almighty
One.

Christians are members of a great fellowship of

reconciliation which leads to cooperation, and group strengthening. This type of victory is superior to domination, compromise, or integration. Compromise and integration may be used in reconciliation between members who have been at odds with each other or who have different ideas concerning a problem. Of all the strategies of intervention, domination is the least productive for individual growth and development, however, with the very young and inadequate person it may be necessary to tell him what to do and how to do it until he is able to function by himself.

(3) Duties and Activities

Konopka has classified the activities of the group worker in the following scheme:

I. Accepting (by a worker or person, feelings, ideas, or behavior)
II. Relating
   A. Member or group to worker
   B. Member or group to member
   C. Member to group
III. Enabling and Supporting
   A. Individuals or group to accept self or others
   B. Individuals or group to
      1. express themselves
      2. accomplish (or have feeling of accomplishment)
   C. Individuals or groups to involve themselves in:
      1. activity (program)
      2. decision making
      3. assuming and carring responsibilities
   D. Individuals and group to gain insight, understanding and security

IV. Limiting behavior that is
   A. Harmful to others and self
   B. Destructive to property and material,

or to relationships
- V. Guiding of discussions, activities and group movement
- VI. Alleviating
  - A. Tension
  - B. Conflict
  - C. Fear and anxiety, or guilt
- VII. Interpreting
  - A. Function of group-worker-agency
  - B. Individual's or group's behavior or feelings
- VIII. Observing and Evaluating (diagnostic appraisal)
  - A. Individual behavior
  - B. Individual's effect on group
  - C. Group behavior
  - D. Worker's effect on individual or group (own practice)
- IX. Planning and Preparing (by worker)
  - A. Group formation and composition
  - B. Program
  - C. Treatment or service[1]


## Tools in Programming

The basic tools in programming are the workers'
warm, purposeful, accepting, non-judgmental attitude,
understanding, and the professional relationship between
the worker and the group member. The worker in turn influences interpersonal relationship among group members--
the group itself. The informal periods of conversation--
just talking to each other and the experiences members
have together which transmit trust and mutual respect are
powerful tools. Other major tools are the use of community resources and creating an atmosphere conducive for
purposeful individual and group development.

---

[1]Konopka, Social Group Work: A Helping Process,
pp. 164-65.

After the emotional stage is set the group can use many interesting and challenging techniques to stimulate wider participation among the members. Group meetings should vary in type and procedure. The purposes of the group and the type of members will determine the tools to be used in programming. The following ideas may be helpful:

1. Discussion groups which increase member-member interaction and mutual help.

A teenage club group in a church program complained about the rules and restrictions imposed on them by the teachers at school. "The teachers were absolutely unreasonable." Sue said, "The school treats us like babies when we are 'thirteen' years old." "We'll be sent home or picked up if we don't give in," said Olivia. "You can't please them. We can't do anything to please," Juanita said as she bit her fingernails.

The group worker asked if they knew why all the rules were made at school. "No, do you know?" was their reply. The worker explained that some girls had cut school and were picked up by the police. The demands of the aroused parents caused the school to tighten up on the rules. The angry girls were more disturbed than ever. The worker said that there were some things which the girls could do about it if they thought it through and made some plans. The girls became less emotional as they talked together.

The next meetings were filled with the girls eval-
ating their feelings and writing out why they objected
to the rules, discussing this with fellow group members
and their parents, and reporting back to the group.
They talked with the school teachers and the principal.
They were very much surprised to have interested list-
eners, and a suggestion that they write out their
suggestions and present them to the principal the
following week.

This was a learning experience which was of mutual
benefit to the teenagers and to the school. The inner
growing-up was beneficial to the individuals and the
group. The group worker fulfilled her responsibility
and showed her skill in allowing expression of both
negative and positive feelings and providing an outlet
for their expressions to be followed up by positive
actions. She was skillful in bringing action into the
entire group.

2. "Activities, doing things together (or alone,
when one needs this), allow for much expression, for
identification with people whom one admires and needs,
for a feeling of accomplishment, for 'telling' without
words."[1]

Activities may also lead to discovery, problem

---

[1]Konopka, Social Group Work: A Helping Process,
p. 131.

solving, locating Scripture, leading to a survey, or
opening a way of getting rid of pent-up feelings.
Three boys, ages 5, 6, and 8 were in a church day care
center. Their father was in the "pen" for misconduct.
The mother worked hard but neglected the children.
They felt unloved and unwanted. Each day as they came
to the center they were acting out in their behavior.
A punching bag was provided and these three little boys
used it to rid themselves of inner feelings. After a
work out they settled down to play with other children
and were contented. The time spent hitting the bag
without a word spoken met their need.

Often groups may have an interplay between doing
something with their hands, talking to others, express-
ing feelings, and learning a new skill. If the worker
watches and listens a great deal can be learned about
the group members.

Activities may be tools to give some status to an
individual in the group. A boy who excels in ball
playing, or one who is skilled in music, art, or drama,
gains acceptance in the group. A boy who spoke a
different language, such as German, spoke up for some
other boys when they were in trouble and gained their
friendship.

Music, drama, puppet play, role playing, prayer
Scripture search, listening to records, books, looking

at pictures, debate, exhibits, trips, buzz groups, panels, problem solving, assignment-reporting, hobbies, research, storytelling, asking questions, talking, arts and crafts, games, talent shows, parties, food, educational programs, and community service projects are some other program activities.

3. Creative use of environment or setting the stage for the group is very important. A group worker met with eight-year-old children in a club after school. They were tired from being in school. The room was set up with a number of interests from which they chose their activity. They felt free to play for about thirty minutes. Then the worker called them into a small group. They sat in a semi-circle with the worker, ate cookies, drank fruit juic, and talked about their plans for the next meeting. Physical setting had a psychological effect upon the group. The club emblem (Shining Stars) was always hanging on the wall in "their" room. This gave them much pride in belonging to the club.

4. Slides, tapes, films, and filmstrips are excellent means for stimulating experiences such as enjoyment of beauty, depicting mission needs, worship, and other worthwhile experiences.

# CHAPTER III

## DAY OR NIGHT CHILD CARE

The purpose of day or night care of children is to provide a home-like atmosphere for children whose mothers work or for children who have special needs. Often children through age twelve are admitted. Admission policies vary greatly, but the plan should stretch to meet the needs of the children.

## Starting Child Care Services

1. Determine the need

See Chapter I, Section on understanding the community.

2. Finances

A large number of church child care services are self-supported through the fees for the care. Some supplement the service through the regular church budget or through persons or groups paying a scholarship for a child to help finances. Some churches charge a regular fee for child care services, while others have a sliding scale plan of charging according to the weekly salary of parent or parents. A sample is included toward the end of this chapter. There should be a financial plan sufficient for salaries, oper-

56

ting costs, insurance, publicity, and needed equipment, and
upplies, retirement plan for workers, and staff in-service
raining.

3. Licensing

Each state has policies which govern the procedure
or starting child care. The best policy is to contact the
ocal Child Welfare Department licensing supervisor for
uidance in meeting the requirements for floor space, equip-
ent, and other policies required for obtaining a license.
facility must be approved by the health department and the
ire department before licensed. These are reviewed annually.
copy of minimum standards from the state department of child
elfare lists the criteria for licensing.

An isolation room, although not always required, is a
rotection for all children in child care **away from** their homes.
his can also serve as an examination room for any child be-
oming ill during the time he is in attendance.

4. Program for Child Care

The children spend the time in natural processes of
ating, sleeping, and playing under a happy, healthly atmos-
here. Physical care includes: a physical examination be-
ore admission; morning health inspection; inoculation and
accination for certain diseases; proper diet, sleeping
abits, and exercise. Adequate equipment should be provided
or indoor and outdoor activities. Many child care centers
ave a program similar to a nursery school.

Educational guidance should be provided for personal hygiene and toileting, self-service habit formation, creative experiences, aesthetic development, social adjustment, muscular-training and development, indoor and outdoor play, eating and sleeping, and habit training. A morning and afternoon snack with a well-balanced lunch are provided. Bible stories, music, art, drama, and many other experiences should be provided for the children. The schedule should be flexible, but should include the above activities and other varied experiences for the total physical, mental, emotional and spiritual development. Free time as well as guided periods are needed.

There should be a full-time supervisor for child care. There is a great deal involved in keeping the medical records, as well as other records. Workers who work directly with children should have formal or practical training and experience. A health card is required of all workers to insure the best protective services for the children. The personality and character of the worker should be suited to the type of work. The group of children should be small and no worker should be expected to be with a group of children for long hours without a break. There should be different shifts of workers so that the hours of work are not over eight hours. Many child care centers open at six in the morning and few close before six o'clock in the evening. Personal experience has shown that mothers of the community who have done a good job with their own children may make

58

excellent nursery workers.

Even though the day care program is informal there must be careful planning on the part of the staff to meet the needs of the children. Each experience should contribute to making the child feel wanted, needed, secure, and adequate. Specific experiences and activities should be planned for each basic learning experience. The following plan may serve as an idea for specific planning.

| Learnings | Experiences | Resources |
|---|---|---|
| Being happy away from home | Visit nursery before entering to know workers, building and materials | Staff, building, equipment and materials |
| Feeling secure | Bring a doll or toy from home to help bridge the gap from home to day care. Seeing all of the rooms | Happy teachers, peer group, personal things and a place for them |
| Making friends | Being introduced to workers and children being treated as a real person | Friendly teachers and children Free atmosphere |
| To discover | Exploring and watching for self the building, play, materials, persons | Trustful teachers and peers, rooms, equipment, etc. |
| Learning about God, Jesus, and others | Meet the pastor, listen to stories, sing, pray, meet new friends | Persons, Bible, books, music, etc. |

Learnings should be planned for all areas of development--habits, attitudes, health and welfare, intellectual, social, moral, emotional, and spiritual.

## Play Materials for Special Purposes

For Development through Age Two:

Animals, soft or wood
Assorted sizes of balls
Water toys, sink
Large beads to string
Blocks--large cardboard or wooden
Nested blocks--square, cone
Wall mirror
Bells, rhythm band equipment, piano, record player,
TV
Books, pictures
Washable dolls of different races, carriage
Hammer toys--pounding toys
Peg boards
Push--pull toys, wagon
Swing, slide
Steps, climbing apparatus, ladder
Wooden trains, trucks, cars
Spoons, rattlers, pail, shovel, sand
Rocking boat, rocking chair
Tricycle
Easel, paint brushes, large crayon, water colors,
newsprint
Doll bed and other furniture, broom and other
housekeeping equipment
Educational puzzle (1 to 3 pieces)
Colored construction paper, blunt scissors
Paste, chalk, telephone
Rope
Clothes basket, iron, ironing board
Cot, blanket, comb, clothes rack, toothbrush, wash-
cloth, soap, paper towels

For Development from Two to Age Six:
In addition to those listed before

Balance board
Beanbags, bubble pipes
Scooters
Throwing toys, wheelbarrow, packing boxes
Barrels, kegs, sieves
Clay, building materials
Sawhorses, worktable, hammer, nails, saws, jigsaw,
rule, wood
Pets
Scales, chalkboard, crayon
Wooden alphabet
Paper sacks, paper plates, pictures

Bulletin board, cash register
Finger paint
Cartons, cans, ribbons, cloth
Puzzles (4-12 pieces)
Scrap book, puppets, screens
Tinker toys, circus set, play costumes
Soap, bubble pipes, counting games
Boy people, animals, houses to build
Airplanes, airport, fire engine, ambulance
Doll, doll clothes, dishes
Garage, gas station, oil truck, dump truck, tractor
Kitchen utensils, toy stove
Tents, villages, boats
Punching bag

For Development from Six to Age Twelve:
In addition to those listed

Balls, baseball, bat, tennis, football, basketball
Marbles, jacks, etc.
Croquet set
Target games, dart games, gym equipment
Geography, math, history and quiz games
Ping pong, toss games, horseshoes
Roller skates, stilts, sleds
Swimming equipment
Swing, hoops, kites
Tumbling equipment
Track--jumping, relays
Weaving looms
Leather craft, paper mache
Whittling, woodburning set
National dolls, scout equipment
Toy piano, world globe
Plant craft, rock gardens
Table games, microscope
Bicycle, shuffleboard
Camping equipment, make-up kits
Printing press, sewing materials
Architectural set, science set
Astronomy set, maps
Bird house building material
Butterfly, shell and insect collection
Camera, coin and stamp collection
Compass, field glasses
Electric train, travel games
Typewriter

# SLIDING SCALE PLAN OF FEES FOR DAY CARE

| NET INCOME WEEKLY | | TOTAL FAMILY UNIT | | | | |
|---|---|---|---|---|---|---|
| | | 2 | 3 | 4 | 5 | 6 |
| $ 25.00 or less | | $ 2.50 | $ 2.50 | $ 2.50 | $ 2.50 | $ 2.50 |
| 25.00 to 30.00 | | 2.75 | 2.75 | 2.75 | 2.75 | 2.75 |
| 30.00 to 35.00 | | 3.25 | 3.00 | 2.75 | 2.75 | 2.75 |
| 35.00 to 40.00 | | 3.50 | 3.25 | 3.00 | 2.75 | 2.75 |
| 40.00 to 45.00 | | 4.00 | 3.50 | 3.25 | 3.00 | 3.00 |
| 45.00 to 50.00 | | 4.50 | 4.30 | 4.20 | 4.10 | 4.00 |
| 50.00 to 55.00 | | 5.00 | 4.80 | 4.70 | 4.60 | 4.50 |
| 55.00 to 60.00 | | 5.50 | 5.30 | 5.20 | 5.10 | 5.00 |
| 60.00 to 65.00 | | 6.00 | 5.80 | 5.70 | 5.60 | 5.50 |
| 65.00 to 70.00 | | 6.50 | 6.30 | 6.20 | 6.10 | 6.00 |
| 70.00 to 75.00 | | 7.00 | 6.80 | 6.70 | 6.60 | 6.50 |
| 75.00 to 80.00 | | 7.50 | 7.30 | 7.20 | 7.10 | 7.00 |
| 80.00 to 85.00 | | 8.00 | 7.80 | 7.70 | 7.60 | 7.50 |
| 85.00 to 90.00 | | 8.50 | 8.30 | 8.20 | 8.10 | 8.00 |
| 90.00 to 95.00 | | 9.00 | 8.80 | 8.70 | 8.60 | 8.50 |
| 95.00 to 100.00 | | 9.50 | 9.30 | 9.20 | 9.10 | 9.00 |
| 100.00 and up | | 10.00 | 9.80 | 9.70 | 9.60 | 9.50 |

NOTE: WHEN TWO OR MORE CHILDREN IN ONE FAMILY ARE ENROLLED
IN THE NURSERY, THE FEE FOR THE FIRST CHILD IS THE
SAME AS FOR AN ONLY CHILD AND THE FEE FOR EACH OTHER
CHILD ENROLLED SHALL BE ONE HALF THE FEE FOR THE
FIRST CHILD (FOR EXAMPLE--IN THE FIRST PRICE LIST, T
FIRST CHILD'S FEE IS $2.50 THE OTHER WOULD BE HALF T
2.50 OR $1.25).

THE FEE MAY VARY FROM WEEK TO WEEK ACCORDING TO WEEK
SALARY. IT IS PAID AT THE BEGINNING OF EACH WEEK.

## DAY CARE MEDICAL STATEMENT

Child's Name_____ Date of Examination_____
                          Birthdate_____ Mo._____ Yr.____
Has been examined by me and found free of infectious and co
tagious disease, and is physically and mentally able to par
ticipate in group activities. Has had the following immu-
nizations:

Diptheria_____ Whooping Cough_____
Tetanus_____ Polio_____
Smallpox_____ Others_____
Any special recommendations_____
_____
Physician's Signature_____
Address_____
Phone_____

5. Staff--Schedules and Suggested Duties for
Nursery Workers

DIRECTOR:

a. Do administrative work in planning with
welfare department, board, etc.

b. Be responsible for policies of operation,
financial plans, and work with teachers,
parents, and children for the interest and
good of all programs, discipline, assign-
ment of jobs.

c. Keep medical records of expenditures, plan
meals, and refreshments, buy groceries, and
guide the educational program.

d. Hold weekly staff meetings and other meetings for workers--continuing in-service
training.

e. Work with teachers on specific duties and
assignments.

f. Conduct class meetings with parents and
keep in touch with parents.

g. Help in counseling when needed--children
and parents.

SECRETARY:

a. Register through the office all children
and help with orientation of parents and
children.

b. Collect nursery fees and help with book-
keeping and correspondence.

c. Make appointments with directors and parents, when necessary.

d. Inspect children and accept them in the
morning.

e. Give first-aid when needed through the day.

f. Help with the children and general nursery
work, when needed.

g. Check roll each day and help keep records.

63

HEAD NURSERY TEACHER:

  a.  Directly responsible for welfare of childre
      Work with other teachers in making decision
      with regard to matters that affect the grou

  b.  Bring special needs to the attention of the
      director.

  c.  Supervise the housekeeping and upkeep of
      equipment. When toys are in need of re-
      pair, ask some worker to care for it, or
      call attention to the director.

  d.  Plan and have charge of music period or
      other as agreed upon by the staff.

  e.  Have general oversight over the nursery,
      keeping bath tissue, paper towels, and
      other necessities on hand at all times,
      and everything clean and orderly.

  f.  Have oversight over meals and refreshments.

ASSISTANT TEACHERS:

  a.  Have responsibility for health and welfare
      of children.

  b.  Work with others to keep building clean and
      everything in order.

  c.  Help wherever needed when children are asle

  d.  Supervise children at play.

  e.  Supervise children as they wash hands for
      refreshments and lunch.

  f.  Help keep play equipment in place, repaired
      and stored over week ends, when necessary.

  g.  Fix sheets on cots each day.

  h.  Take sheets and blankets off cots after
      naps for laundry.

  i.  Assist with story hour each morning.

  j.  Attend staff meetings and other meetings to
      learn how to be more effective.

    k.  Read good literature on work with children
         to improve self and work.

    l.  Be in charge of one group of children for
         outdoor play, indoor play.

    m.  Help out in any area in case of emergency.

COOK AND MAID SERVICE:

    a.  Prepare wholesome meal and refreshments.

    b.  Keep kitchen clean and in good order.

    c.  Keep self clean and meet health standards.

    d.  Do special agreed upon duties with regard
         to cleanliness of nursery.

    e.  Be careful to follow directions in prepara-
         tion, serving, and storing goods immediately
         after lunch.

6.  Some Ways in Which Parents May Cooperate

    a.  Have a conference with the Director before
         child enters the Child Care Facility so that
         you may see the facilities and discuss en-
         rollment procedures.

    b.  No child will be admitted until all required
         record blanks are completed.

    c.  Children must be vaccinated for whooping
         cough, typhoid and small pox, and immunized
         against diptheria before they may be enrolled
         in the Nursery.  A doctor's statement of
         health must be brought.  (This statement must
         be renewed yearly, stating the child is free
         of infectious diseases).  Bring vaccination
         certificate.  A doctor's statement when en-
         rolling child or when readmitting him after
         he has had a communicable disease is re-
         quired.

    d.  Work schedule of parent or parents and the
         date pay is received must be given.

    e.  Children are to be brought to the Center
         only when the mothers are at work, unless
         this is approved by the director.

f.  Parents must not leave children any day
    until examined by the teacher in charge.

g.  Children should be kept at home on days
    when they show any of the following
    symptoms:  sore throat, running nose,
    cough, fever, rash, earache or headache.

h.  Parents will be called to take children
    home if they are found to be ill while in
    day or night care.

i.  Promptly notify the Center of child's ill-
    ness or any problem which calls for him to
    be absent.  When a child returns to the
    Nursery after absence for any cause, give
    reason for his absence.

j.  See that all clothing is marked with child's
    name.

k.  Each child must keep two extra suits of
    underclothing and one extra dress or suit
    in the Nursery.

l.  Discussion of child with teachers should be
    done when the child is not present.  Make
    appointments for conferences with the direc-
    tor or the head teacher.

m.  Attend parents' meetings.

n.  Remember the Nursery schedule.  Child should
    be picked up within 30 minutes after parent
    gets off work.

o.  Give names of persons who may call for the
    child.

p.  Fees must be paid one week in advance.  The
    full fee is paid for attendance of three or
    more days; 2/5 of the weekly fee for two
    days attendance and 1/5 for one day.  An
    extra 25¢ per child is charged for each half
    hour over time to be picked up.

q.  Parents help to provide a happier and safer
    place for the children by participating with
    the teachers in planning them.

# BIBLIOGRAPHY FOR CHILD CARE WORKERS

A BLIND CHILD TOO, CAN GO TO NURSERY SCHOOL, Pauline M. Moor, American Foundation for the Blind, 15 W. 16th Street, New York, New York, 10011, 1952

A CREATIVE GUIDE FOR PRESCHOOL TEACHERS, Joanne Wylie, Western Publishing Company, Inc., Whitman Hobby Division Department M, 1220 Mound Avenue, Racine, Wisconsin, 53404

DIBS IN SEARCH OF SELF, Virginia M. Axline, Houghton Mifflin Company, Boston, Massachusetts, 1964

EDUCATION IN THE KINDERGARTEN, Josephine C. Foster and Neith E. Headley, American Book Company, 55 Fifth Avenue, New York, New York, 10003, 1948

FUN COMES FIRST FOR BLIND SLOW-LEARNERS, Mildred Blake Huffman, Charles C. Thomas, Publisher, 301 East Lawrence Avenue, Springfield, Illinois, 62703, 1957

GRADED BIBLE CLUBS FOR THE CHURCH, Alpha Melton, Available from Southwestern Baptist Theological Seminary, Box 22277, Fort Worth, Texas, 76122, 1969

LANGUAGE FOR THE PRESCHOOL DEAF CHILD, Grace M. Harris, Grune and Stratton, Inc., 381 Park Avenue S, New York, New York, 10016, 1963

NURSERY SCHOOL PORTFOLIO AND KINDERGARTEN PORTFOLIO, Association for Childhood Education International, 3615 Wisconsin Avenue, Washington, D.C., 20016

THE CHURCH'S MINISTRY IN MENTAL RETARDATION, Harold W. Stubblefield, Broadman Press, 127 Ninth Avenue N., Nashville, Tennessee, 37203, 1965

THE EXCEPTIONAL CHILD, Walter B. Barbe, The Center for Applied Research in Education, Inc., Washington, D.C., 20000, 1963

THE NURSERY SCHOOL: A HUMAN RELATIONSHIPS LABORATORY, Katherine H. Read, W. B. Saunders Company, 218 W. Washington Square, Philadelphia, Pennsylvania, 19105, 1950

WINNING THE CHILDREN, Gaines Dobbins, Broadman Press, 127 Ninth Avenue N, Nashville, Tennessee, 37203, 1953

CHAPTER IV

OTHER SCIENTIFIC METHODS

There are many methods and techniques in the profession of social work which may be adapted and used in a
church. Social case work, which is helping persons with
problems one-to-one or in groups such as a family, has been
used for many years in some churches. The concept of counseling with the family together has come into practice
within the last few years and is effective under capable
leadership. Community planning is another method which is
useful for the church. This book will not deal with these
methods except as they relate to working with groups.
Chapter II has referred to making use of a community study
to determine needs for a week day ministry. Many of the
group work principles discussed in Chapter III are applicabl
in work with individuals as well as in community planning.

This chapter will deal with some of the group work
techniques which the author has observed, used, or knows
are of value in reaching individuals and helping them to
solve problems through groups. Simple illustrations are
given. The different techniques which are included are:

Techniques for Treatment Through Activity Groups
Help for the Aging
Help for Mentally Retarded

68

Treating Groups Through Education
    T- Group
    Patterning
Recognizing and Helping Persons with Common Problems
    Help with Spiritual Problems
    Help with Emotional Problems
Special Techniques for Bringing About Behavior Change

## Techniques for Treatment Through
### Activity Groups

Using groups in the church is a common practice. In the early New Testament churches groups were close-knit fellowships which shared what they had and identified with each other to the extent that the group experiences served as spiritual, emotional, and social therapy for the group members.

Social scientists have had great interest in group work which has become one of the primary methods of the social work profession. In the field of education the concept of learning by doing is well accepted. The author has personally found that activities in the small, as well as large group, are powerful for inducing learning and promoting growth or change in attitudes and behavior, when the aims and purposes are specified. Activity for activity's sake may have little value, while activity with a purpose in mind can produce amazing results. Activity groups should be functional. They may be thought of as the interaction between two or more persons, in pursuit of desired goals which meet the needs of the participants.

The types of activity will vary according to the needs and purposes of the group. Some activities, if done purposefully may produce the following:

- Opportunity for creative expression - individual growth

- Provision for acceptance, enjoyment, and satisfaction

- Developing and using talents and skills

- Developing self awareness

- Productive thinking - recognition of individual potential

- Changing habits or behavior

- Rehabilitation of persons - physically, mentally, emotionally, socially, and/or spiritually

- Interpersonal relationship experiences

Churches may be creative and find and use many more purposeful activities than are ordinarily found. Arts and crafts have varied uses but are often overworked because of a lack of creativity on the part of leaders. The use of arts and crafts may be effective for individual growth, provision for creative expression, enjoyment and satisfaction, developing or using talents and skills and is often a means of rehabilitation of persons - physically, mentally, emotionally, and socially. Observation reveals that many churches in their overuse of crafts may really stifle the imagination of the participants.

## Help for the Aging

About three years ago, the author was given the priviledge of doing creative group work with older adults. There were about forty ladies who regularly attended a

70

"Tuesday Club." All of them brought some food to add to the "covered-dish" luncheon. The meeting lasted four to five hours, including the luncheon. After lunch the groups participated in self-chosen activities which included table games, service projects, viewing films, and crafts.

Within the large group there were about fifteen ladies who were observed to be non-participants except for the luncheon. They would sit at tables as far away from the "center" of the group as possible. They talked very little and this was only to those sitting by them at the luncheon table. Upon observation, it was felt that their minds and total personalities were deteriorating. It seemed that the "blinds had been pulled" and these persons had nothing to live for - so they just waited for death.

An opportunity was presented to the large group for those who might be interested in planning and participating in something new and creative that they would do as a group. Fifteen persons came to the first meeting. Later, others joined the group. It was suggested that this group was not to do anything that was already being done, but the group was free to be creative - use their own ability to think what they would like to do together. "This" group was being formed to encourage individuality, ingenuity, free expression,and independence so that their program would be unlike any other.

It was amazing how surprised but free the members were as they recognized that they were being trusted and

71

challenged to use their minds, talents, and skills when they had just gone along with the large group with its leaders who seemed unconcerned about them. They were being given an opportunity to clearly and creatively think what they wanted to do. They felt "we must be important."

The group considered that they wanted a program in which each member could participate. Then, they began thinking of the talents of each individual. They were to express wants, thoughts, and actions to achieve the best for the group. After sitting through the luncheon and general business and program of the larger club, they were tired and ready for a change in activity. They needed relaxation and to have some fun together.

After discussion the group decided to organize a household band and to work together so that they might put on a program for the entire club group. It was interesting to see some of the ones who had seemed to mentally deteriorate spring back into action and reveal an entirely different personality. This simple activity, with no cost to the group, proved to be a rewarding experience for each person. The members became creative thinkers with personality-plus as they practiced and put on a program which became known throughout the city.

The plastic waste baskets with wooden spoons and tin pans became drums; a cake pan with plastic scraper took on new meaning; clusters of measuring spoons rang forth; teaspoons with water glasses holding graduated amounts of water

72

added beauty; a toy wash board with the eraser end of a
pencil sounded out the rhythmic count of time; the Dover
egg beater swished a clear note; hair combs with tissue
paper set the tune along with other "instruments."

The performance before the large club was so good
that it was discussed by some non-members of the large
group that the band should be advertised so that it could
perform in other places and on TV.

What made the simple activity so important was not
the activity itself but the effect that the planning and
participation had upon the group members.  Personality
changes were brought about because the members were being
and doing something rewarding, regularly with a group,
with a purpose clearly in mind.  It also gave them something to think about besides themselves.  They often practiced alone at home and called me on the telephone to talk
and to tell of "new instruments" they had discovered.  They
had a challenge which resulted in less worrying about
yesterday, today, and tomorrow which always tends to lead
to neurosis.  They developed integrity by being dependable,
responsibility by being creative and industrious, and other
traits by pursuing their group goals.  They became more
interesting, developed new friends, and proved that they were
still capable, in spite of the fact that some were past
seventy-five in age.  They received blessings and became a
blessing to others.

73

## Help for the Mentally Retarded

Another <u>purposeful activity</u> which blessed the lives
of group members as well as persons outside the group was
that of a "home visit." The small group was made up of
teenage girls who lived in a school for retarded children.
Two of the girls had never been in a "home." As the author
worked with this group and learned of this problem, one of
the first <u>goals</u> was to get the group into someone's home.

A friend in a small church with the assistance of
some other ladies invited the group to a luncheon in her
beautiful home. Many activities such as discussion and
role playing were used to prepare these socially deprived
girls for this new experience. The big day came to visit
in a home and have lunch. The girls were all clean and
neatly dressed. We drove the forty miles in a "State" car.
On the trip there was great joy and expectation. It was
rewarding to see how these girls, with little or no social
experiences, such as this, could have such a good time and
behave in such a socially acceptable way. The greatest
excitement for the two who were so deprived was seeing a
bedroom with only one bed and seeing a bathroom with only
one commode. What these girls had known was a ward in an
institution with rows of beds and in the bathroom rows of
commodes.

This was the first of several such purposeful
experiences for these girls. The last experience which was

74

planned for this group by this group worker was "eating out" at a large restaurant. This was after the author had worked with the group for more than six months. It was rewarding to the members, as well as to the worker, for them to select their own meal as the worker read the menus.

All of the feelings were not rewarding. As Christians in various places have experienced or heard of the depravity and of the opportunities for service to even those who know the least, there is a feeling of shame because the church has done such a little in service to the retarded, as well as to many other groups of people who are lonely, unwanted, and neglected. Our example in Jesus will cry out that He never lost sight of any individual in need and God is looking to all Christians everywhere to <u>look</u>, <u>see</u>, and <u>do</u> in His Name that the frustrated world may learn of Him and His great love and power.

## Treating Groups Through Education

There are countless ways to help groups through general education as well as through religious education. There are two distinct ways discussed here which are simple and useful but may be the least known by lay church members.

### T-Group

The T-Group (Training Group) is an experience-based learning method. Participants work and share together in a small group composed of ten to fifteen people. The sessions

usually vary in length from eight to forty hours. The time
may be planned all together, be in blocks of time, or sched-
uled over a long period of time. There may be a single small
group or several small laboratory groups meeting at the same
time with some sessions together. The together sessions may
be used to present theories, case studies, films, inter-
group experiences, role playing, and other information of
interest to the entire group.

The T-Group was started about 1947 by the National
Training Laboratories. Its purpose was to educate adults
in group dynamics and interpersonal relationships. Today
this laboratory experience is used in a variety of settings
for many different purposes. The key purpose of the group
is to learn. The group itself presents varied or similar
experiences to group members which forms the basis for
learnings for others within the group. Experiences of relationships among and between group members are studied
and brought out.

There is a trainer or resource person who leads the
group to recognize that they build up their own group life
and work. No agenda is prescribed and there is no designated chairman. The group has frustrating, but challenging
experiences as they agree on what to do, how to do it, and
evaluate to see how each coped with a situation or how he
contributed to different and sometimes difficult or traumatic tasks. The experience helps in learning how groups

76

ork and each individual becomes aware of himself and how
e functions.

Honesty and trust are very important. Openness
egarding positive and negative feelings, behavior, skills,
elf-awareness, self-confidence, purposes, and such like
re discussed. How one's feelings and behavior affect him
nd how they affect others are frankly brought out. It may
e traumatic for one to tell another in the presence of the
roup that he is not telling the truth or that he is so
elf-centered that he is not accepted; however, if he can
ecome aware of himself and how he affects others, he will
uffer but will bring about changes in his behavior.

This T- (training) Group technique can best be
nderstood through a simple illustration. A small group of
bout fifteen high school girls in a classroom situation
ecided that they wanted to have a genuine growth and devel-
pment experience. They decided to be honest with each
ther and help each other become aware of their problems so
nat with the help of the group they could experience change.

Within a two hour laboratory session, the girls be-
an to study each other. They lived in the same neighbor-
ood so they knew each other. One girl said,"S., you are
lways late to almost everything you attend." S. might not
ave liked this openness, but the girls had agreed that this
as an experience they wanted, so she admitted to this prob-
em. Another girl said to M., "You tell a falsehood when

the truth would fit better."  Another said,"A., you gossip
and tell everything you know about others."  "K.,you blow
your stack everytime things don't go like you want them to
go."  This frankness went on for some time.

The next week at another session each girl would
tell how she was trying to cope with her problem.  Sometimes another would give support by saying, "I had that
problem and I did thus and so."  K. said, "I almost 'blew
my stack' at home, but I thought of our plan and I held bac
M. said, "I almost told a lie to someone but I thought of
our plan and decided to tell the truth."

This learning experience develops a sense of self-
understanding which is basic to living a fuller and more
victorious life.  Churches across the country have used
such techniques known by various names, such as encounter
groups, confrontation groups, renewal groups, and others.
The purpose is to work together for a higher degree of
personal integrity, self-awareness, and development.

The plan is not outlined for the group but it seems
to bear out the idea of the following:  1) becoming more
aware of individual problems; 2) through suffering because
of actual confrontation of the problem, working out for
oneself a solution; 3) getting with it to be an "overcomer
and because of the nature of the group, 4) after confrontation giving and/or getting support to fellow group members
in their struggles to gain victory over their problems.

t is experiencing for growth and development. This tech-
ique might not be used with serious personality problems.

It seems to the author that such a simple plan is
ppropriate for many church groups and is biblical because
f admonitions to confess sins to one another (James 5:16),
he strong are to help the weak (Romans 15:1), one is to
ear another's burdens (Galatians 6:2), and one is not to
udge another lest he be judged (Matt. 7:1).

## Patterning to Help Brain
## Damaged Children

This is a therapy (treatment) which is of recent
rigin. It is controversial and unconventional. It is
sually thought of as the Doman-Delacato method - named
fter two men, Robert Doman, an M.D., and Carl H. Delacato,
n Ed.D. The whole idea is to remove the learning barriers
n the brain. It is a treatment patterned after the physi-
al movements of an infant of turning the head and moving
he arms and legs. The brain damaged child is unable to do
he normal exercises so the therapists do them to and for
im.

As the author observed these simple and interesting
xercises being performed by women of a church she was
mazed at the self-giving of the ladies to help mentally de-
rived children. Even though there are many who are skep-
ical of the method, the author was caught by the enthusiasm
f some mothers of brain damaged children which will be

79

presented in brief a little later on in this discussion.

The plan is to place a child on a padded table which is high enough for the workers (therapists) to be comfortable at work. An ordinary table may be raised by fitted lifts for the table legs to elevate the table to counter height. A pad could be laid on the table. The child is placed on his stomach. There needs to be from three to five workers - one at the head, one for each arm and one for each leg. The exercises must be rhythmic. This was accomplished by a worker at the head (the patterner) counting to establish rhythm. As the head is turned to the right, the right arm and right leg are bent at elbow and knee and brought up. When the head is turned to the left the left arm and left leg are bent and brought up. The patterners at the arms and feet grasp the wrist or ankle with one hand and the knee or elbow with the other hand. This assures bending and raising the arm or leg as the head is turned. This is done rhythmically as a clock ticks for five minutes per session. There are four sessions each morning at 30 minutes apart. The worker controlling the head should be careful to protect the face so that no injury occurs. After each patterning, the child is put on the floor and is helped to crawl, creep, or walk. Pictures are used to stimulate talking and reading when they are ready for this. (A diagram of patterning is available from: Institutes for the Achievement of Human Potential,

8801 Stenton Avenue, Philadelphia 18, Pa.)

It is found advantageous to have as little conversation as possible, no music or TV program, and no crying
of other children while the patterning is being done.  Before children are entered into this program it is necessary
for them to have a complete medical examination.  There
should be a doctor and someone trained to evaluate
the progress of each child as the program proceeds.

The patterning sessions which I observed had been
in progress for over three years in the church.  The
schedule was from nine to eleven o'clock each morning
Monday through Friday.  The therapists were lady volunteers
who care and give their time, love, and energy to the helpless.  Some of the ladies had brain damaged children.
Several mothers told of children who had been helped so
that they could live a normal life.  The IQ is often raised
through patterning exercises.

One three-year-old child before treatment had three
or four seizures each week and after six months of patterning they have been reduced to three or four a month.  She
never laughed, never recognized or responded to parents or
to anything, she could not crawl, creep, or walk.  Now after
six months she responds to cuddling, smiles and has begun to
crawl on her stomach.  Another child in treatment for less
than a year is walking.  Some children learn to read or
improve their reading ability.  The mothers were so pleased

81

to know of some who now ride a bicycle and get along well with other children and adults.

Schools are springing up just for the purpose mentioned here, but where there are no schools churches have a challenge and a responsibility to minister to the whole person. The patterning therapy seems to be an open door of service for retired persons, responsible teenagers and others in the church who need to feel useful and wanted. Instead of laying persons on a shelf or of allowing youth to become bored because of nothing to do, this service can be a blessing to children, to the families, to the "servants" and to the entire church.

One school with which the author is familiar is the University of Plano, located at Plano, Texas. Adult students who are in the developmental education program are required to spend as much as an hour each day patterning on the floor. This is done under supervision. Some of the students are eventually able in addition to reading to take courses such as English, mathematics, and others. Much research is being done with regard to this method with some interesting and positive findings being discovered. If onl a few persons are helped, they deserve the chance to develo to their highest potential.

## Recognizing and Helping Persons
### With Common Problems

It is easy for a church leader to look at every
problem as being a spiritual one. Often Christians say,
"Just pray about it," or "Read the Bible and do what God
says." Some of the greatest Christians have at times had
problems with which they were unable to cope. Some have
problems and do not recognize them. The saddest thing hap-
pens when one Christian judges another and condemns him
when the judged is unconscious of his problem and might respond if some love and skill were put together in his
behalf.

Often an emotional problem leads to a spiritual
problem and vice versa. Physical illness can lead to emotional and spiritual problems. If persons are to be helped
the problems need to be recognized, separated, and dealt with.
It may be that when one problem is resolved another will be
removed or weakened.

### Help with Spiritual Problems

A few days ago a young man, age 25, came to our
house. I had met him at a meeting the week before. My husband had never seen him. He said that he was compelled by
an inner force to come to our home. He told us that he had
left his home state to come to Fort Worth, Texas. He recognized God as one of power who was always with him, and had

83

trusted Jesus as his Savior. In his early life, he had disregarded his body as a vessel of God, but knew that he had the indwelling Spirit of God within him. He felt that he was running away from and was resisting God. He had felt a call to serve God but had not yielded in obedience to him because he did not want to preach.

This young man had had many unusual experiences with regard to direct leadership of God in getting jobs and in protection on many occasions from physical harm. He has a deep love and compassion for people who are in trouble and has a burning desire to help others, especially in the rehabilitation of juvenile delinquents. As he talked to us he kept referring to the fear he had over what was going to happen to him if he did not obey God and get busy doing whatever he wanted him to do. What was his problem? It was basically a spiritual problem which has the potential of causing deep emotional problems. He was conscious of his behavior of disobedience. I feel that he actually wanted to know and do what was right for him. If he continually resists God, he is surely going to feel guilty, may drift away from God failing to have the close, rich, and rewarding experiences which have been his when he feels near the Lord.

Nelson gives six symptoms which will help one to recognize spiritual problems:

1. There exists a lack of desire to think properly, even though there is the ability to do so.

EXAMPLE: Thinking bad thoughts without becoming distressed about them.

EXAMPLE: Not desiring to be willing to obey God, and deliberately rebelling against Him.

2. This involves the area of the will: misbehavior as the result of deliberate disobedience, and not from a lack of self-control. The individual is not sufficiently distressed by his spiritual failure.

EXAMPLE: A person who stubbornly misbehaves sexually because he wants to and has never determined in his mind to try to behave correctly.

3. Conscience may be underdeveloped, perhaps due to ignorance. Or a person may ignore and reject the warnings of his conscience.

EXAMPLE: A person does not feel guilty enough to try to improve his actions; or, he may feel guilty, but represses his guilt and refuses to admit he is violating his conscience.

4. Real motives for misbehavior are usually conscious and the person may have to suffer unpleasant consequences before he becomes willing to change.

EXAMPLE: A person may not even try to stop misbehaving until he begins to suffer unpleasant results. He continues as long as he can get away with it.

5. When the proper spiritual remedy is appropriated the problem is solved.

EXAMPLE: A person's misbehavior ceases when he, as a Christian, adopts the proper spiritual attitude and relies on help from God. Exhortation from other Christians may help.

6. A person is ignorant but can see his problem when he is given clear and sufficient spiritual instruction.

EXAMPLE: A person's problem may disappear when he learns and appropriates a new truth which relates to his problem .[1]

He had never thought of work with juvenile delinquents as a ministry of the Lord. He had missed the fact

---

[1]Marion H. Nelson, M.D., Why Christians Crack Up (Chicago: Moody Press, n.d.), pp. 23-24.

of the Scriptures that some are evangelists, some teachers and some pastors and that God gives talents to one to do one service and to another talents to use to help others and bring glory to God. As we talked and as he read Scriptures he remarked, "I see, that's why I had to come here." After he ate dinner with us he said, "I've never had such peace. I now know where I should go and what I should do. Thank God!" When he saw for himself the spiritual truths in the Scripture he was ready to appropriate them to his life.

This was helping through simple informal, unplanned conversation with openness and leadership of the Holy Spirit. The open Bible on the coffee table was really his answer as he picked it up and thumbed through pointing up some verses to us. It was natural for us to share some Scriptural truths which have been like lighted lamps for us. Many times God uses Christians in very unexpected and unusual ways when they want to be used and whenever He needs to use them.

## Help with Emotional Problems

How can a lay church member recognize and separate from other problems an emotional (psychological) problem? Nelson gives six symptoms which are helpful in recognizing psychological problems.

1. The ability to think logically and to control the thoughts is decreased.

EXAMPLE: An illogical and unrealistic fear which the person does not want to have but which returns repeatedly, causing him distress.

EXAMPLE: An impulse to rebel against God when the person earnestly desires to obey God.

2. Self-control is decreased so that repeated misbehavior results although there is a desire to behave correctly.

EXAMPLE: A person repeatedly misbehaves sexually even though he really tries to behave correctly.

3. Conscience is frequently well developed or even too strict, causing normal or even excessive guilt.

EXAMPLE: Guilt may cause depression that interferes with one's mental ability to improve his behavior.

4. Real motives behind misbehavior may be subconscious and require psychotherapy to bring them to the surface.

EXAMPLE: A person who misbehaves sexually, not out of sexual desire, but due to a subconscious longing for love and attention which was denied him in childhood. He tries to stop, but repeatedly fails.

5. A problem is persistently unresponsive to the usual spiritual remedies (such as prayer, exhortation, etc.).

EXAMPLE: Spiritual failure continues to recur because the basic underlying psychological problem has not been resolved.

6. A person is blind to the fact that he has a problem and repeated efforts to point it out to him meet with defeat.

EXAMPLE: A person cannot seem to "see" the problem because of a mental block. This is evidence of a subconscious reluctance to admit the truth.[1]

Dealing with deep emotional problems may call for community agencies working together. The church as a part of the community has many contributions to make while other agencies

---

[1]Ibid., pp. 23-24.

may have skilled staff to be made use of by the church. There are a great many skills and techniques which are use by lay church members working cooperatively with a trained person in the church or outside the church. Small childre are treated differently to those of later preteen age and older.

Play therapy is a technique which has been very successful in resolving emotional problems of children. T book Dibs In Search of Self listed in Section III Minister in the Classified Bibliography of Resource Material is a simply written book showing treatment by play therapy to a boy who had been in private school for about two years. The child did not talk, had temper tantrums, participated very little except observing and listening, huddled in a corner or moved around on the floor away from others, and was a puzzle to all adults. The skilled worker brings the emotionally ill child to become a whole person with brilliant and creative abilities. An educated person who has mature love and concern and who cares enough to study Dibs and observe play therapy in a hospital or Child Guidance Clinic can become a helper for emotionally disturbed children. The healed child often means a more mentally healthy family.

In my experience many emotionally disturbed childre have been helped. One six-year-old girl who had entered public school was tense with resistance. She refused to lo up. The school referred her to the Child Guidance Clinic

here she was receiving psychiatric help. She remained unresponsive to the help.

The school administrator asked if we would admit her
to kindergarten in the church related week day ministry located near the school. We accepted the challenge to help
the child for we felt that group experiences might meet
her needs. The kindergarten teacher was a warm, accepting,
knowledgeable person with a great deal of patience and
compassion for children.

L. came to kindergarten each morning never lifting
her head. She backed away, huddled against the wall and
sat for days without getting up from her chair. She participated in one activity. She drank milk with the other
children each morning. The teacher and the other children
would present opportunities for activity, but she sat mutely
in her chair. Without pushing, the teacher smiled at her,
patted her on the head and continually expressed love and
acceptance of her as she was.

In visiting L's. home it was soon discovered that
she was not accepted nor treated as a six-year-old child.
She was left in the morning to get her own breakfast and to
look after herself--to be and act like an adult. Both
parents, and the older children worked to try to provide
for the family. They did not realize that money could not
meet emotional needs.

For weeks L. attended kindergarten without any
change. She went weekly to the Child Guidance Clinic. The

89

therapist saw no change in her, however she had seen, heard
and felt, so learning was taking place. After about three
months the teacher put her hand under L's. chin, lifted her
face and looked into her blue eyes and said, "L., you are
beautiful when you hold up your face." This, plus the many
hours of accepting, understanding, honesty, offering opportunities, consistently giving of self, etc., L. became a
whole person. She suddenly began to smile and become a
part of the group. In fact, she became a leader who was of
great help to the teacher. The church kindergarten, school
and Child Guidance Clinic were richly rewarded for their
services. A sick child was made well. She emerged from
her self-imposed withdrawal and isolation. Social development was significant. Any helping process is evaluated
by the consistency and the balance between what a person
brings to the group and what she gets and takes out of the
group. It was not controlling the activities or influences
upon L. that helped, but the fact that she was given opportunities, allowed to assume responsibility as she grew in
ability and came to feel that she was important. She had
to accept and gain her own psychological independence.
The next September L. entered public school and the writer
observed her until she finished elementary school. A
deep satisfaction floods one's soul as he is used of the
Lord in ministering to bring healing to some other human
being. L. had been challenged to recognize that she had
knowledge of her inner world and that responsible freedom

90

to grow and develop was within her. She developed self-respect and a feeling of dignity so that she was able to compete with other children at school. The feeling of security and adequacy spurred her to keep on growing and developing. She had to accept herself as she was and use her own abilities rather than deny them by pushing them back. Children can be helped without involving parents, however, some cases may demand therapy for both.

Strategies for changing the attitudes, feelings, and behavior of preteens and older persons may differ from that used with children. These persons more deliberately make up their mind to seek help. They can be helped so that the problem can be recognized and separated. A plan for overcoming or managing the problem is set up and followed.

The large number of persons needing treatment and the few trained workers available makes vital the outreach of the church to offer effective services. The church may not have enough professionally trained individuals to meet all of the needs but by cooperating with other community agencies it can do much to meet the needs of families within the church neighborhood. Churches have always reached out in time of crises. The crisis theory offers a useful tool in dealing with illness, antisocial behavior, child welfare, personal and family relationship problems.

Crisis is a turning point in a disease, an important decision, a crucial time, stage or situation which is

91

threatening one's life goals, security or affectional ties. The threat caused by the stress seems impossible to solve and overtakes one's ego strength causing uncontrollable tension and anxiety. Life from birth to death poses tension points. Some persons and families are weakened by a stressful experience while others show great strength. Christian psychiatrists are finding that persons who know Jesus Christ as a personal Saviour and live in an abiding relationship with Christ have strength to overcome emotional stress more readily than those who are unbelievers and are without God as Savior and Lord.

There are common types of responses to stressful experiences--anxiety which reveals a threat to some basic need; depression brought on by loss of a loved one because of death, war, divorce, etc; and challenge to use strength for that which is of greater mental, social, and spiritual health. Early life experiences in resolving stress affect later modes of coping with problems. Crises often reactivate early unresolved and hidden problems.

Treating emotional problems may require short or long periods of time. Usually crises of recent development require a shorter time span than do those of long standing. The short term treatment may be done by skilled persons with little professional training, while deep-seated emotional problems require more professional help. The sooner one is helped the better, since true facts are more easily recognized soon after a problem has occurred, because he has not developed ways of gratification or defenses which cover up the real problem. An example of this is a woman with deep emotional problems who developed an intellectual skill of hiding her real problem with showing off intellectually because she felt secure in this area of her life.

The worker begins where the person being helped is. He is an enabler and influencer of change. He thinks of the stress and the problems it evokes in order to motivate the ego forces of the client, of the family, and larger social environment. The worker attempts to deepen awareness of the problem and suggests new ways of coping with the problem to get the client involved in constructive efforts. This calls for the worker to have understanding of normal and abnormal behavior as well as normal and maladaptive reactions to problems causing stress.

Manipulative or mechanistic approaches are often thought of as nil because each person must be treated as a unique individual. Understanding, support, and relief from further tension result in a relationship which is conducive to the helping process.

Family approach to treatment is becoming more accepted. When one member of the family hurts, the entire family hurts; so it seems logical that the best help can be done with the entire family, with probably the very young placed in a nursery during the counseling or treatment sessions.

Family therapy does not exclude helping individuals within the family when there are specific needs. Sessions may be planned for individuals, pairs of members and the entire family. The Family in Dialogue, by A. Donald Bell, Zondervan Publishing House, Grand Rapids, Michigan, 1968, may be helpful in ministering to families.

Family therapy calls for special skills lest the persons be hurt. Family treatment is helpful in case of delinquency, illness, death and many other stressful situations. The real value of working with families is that of recognizing personal identity and of family interaction which plays up defenses used by different members. The worker serves as a social parent, an integrative force to motivate and coordinate all the services. Often he introduces order in the family, helps establish new or altered patterns of reacting and communicating, builds up self-esteem and reduces feelings of unworthiness and helplessness. The worker encourages ventilation of feelings, but helps members become independent, and holds out faith and hope for each one. The worker must be honest, aware of, and willing to face his own feelings as well as those of the family. There must be control and agreed upon limits regarding behavior in the family sessions. There must be an agreement that all are equal and that each is to be involved in trying to understand what led to the crisis and what the family can do to resolve the problem.

Another world-wide problem in which I have been interested for many years is that of understanding and helping battered children and their parents who are batterers. This calls for family treatment. For more than twenty-five years the author has been directly and indirectly involved with these problems. This summer (1969) I attended a seminar at the University of Colorado School of Medicine which dealt with diagnosing and care of the battered child. Battering which is common today includes: physical abuse or neglect, inconsistent treatment, being undernourished, over clean or not clean, continual verbal abuse, expecting too much too soon, deprived of love, sexual abuse and similar physical, mental, emotional, or spiritual abuse or neglect.

As I attended this seminar the thing that impressed me was the team approach of professionals in dealing with the problems. There were pediatricians, psychiatrists, social workers, nurses, lawyers, police, and juvenile probation officers working together to help both children and parents.

Since there is a continually rising rate of child abuse, I feel that Christians have a definite responsibility in regard to this problem. As a church related social worker for the past twenty-five years, the author has been aware of child abuse in many forms. There has been a slow response on the part of many to facing the issue in a scientific, creative, or Christian way. There has often

95

been compassion but too few have been willing to really get involved. Just what can a church do to help in such a serious problem? I would like to make a few practical suggestions regarding the church and what she can do.

. The church can open its doors as a center of concern It can help in the prevention of serious problems by broadcasting "we care about you, here is our address and telephone number." A strong and consistent visitation program can mean much to people who need the church.

. There can be a carefully selected and trained group who can identify the potential batterers. A large number of batterers come from homes where they were battered by their parents, from those who have unrealistic expectations of children, retarded or mentally ill parents, parents with marital problems, and those who have little self-control with regard to alcohol, drugs, etc.

. The church can set up within and without a cooperative team to help parents and children--to cut across the disciplines to involve ministers, educators, nurses, doctors, social workers, and interested lay members. This can be done by working with existing hospitals and other agencies concerned about child welfare.

. Provide educational opportunities for parents on what to expect of children of various age groups, how to be good parents, and similar projects.

- Day care helps relieve the mother and provides needed experience for the child.

- Understand, accept, and demonstrate love. Forget that the problem is child abuse. Think of the parent or child in trouble, probably scared and helpless with low self-esteem. Treat the problem as any other emotional problem.

- Form small therapy groups for parents. The principles of small groups presented in Chapter I and Chapter II of this book and the ideas in the two books listed here may be helpful. Integrity Therapy, John Drakeford, Broadman Press, Nashville, Tennessee, 1967, and the group approaches discussed in Farewell to the Lonely Crowd by John Drakeford, Word Books, Publishers, Waco, Texas, 1969.

- Promote help instead of punishment. Punishing batterers may cause them to be more punishing. They need understanding and acceptance with love which constrains one to help them to handle their feelings. Be open and honest to help them understand what is happening and why. Accept what they say but recognize that they are trying to protect themselves. Focus on them, encourage, build up confidence and self-esteem, involve them, and other agencies to meet their needs. Continue to care, hold on - do not drop them(they have already been rejected too much).

. Promote legislation for child protective services.
Some states require doctors to report child abuse,
but some cases are not seen by doctors. The church
needs to be concerned enough to help prevent "under-
takers" from being the first to know of child neglect
or abuse.

## Bringing about Behavior Change

The thesis behind the socio-behavioral theory, suggested here, is that behavior is learned, therefore it can
be modified or changed. Changing complex behavior is done
through educating a person on how he may alter the situation
which controls his behavior or through planning a program
so that others may influence change in behavior. Behavior
can be acquired, strengthened, maintained, weakened, or
eliminated.

The technique given here is very simple. I have
not given all of the theory or the techniques which may be
employed by therapists. What I want to give is a simple
plan which may be used by lay persons in the church to help
children, youth, and adults who really want help in changing
their patterns of behavior.

There is a great deal of literature on the theory
in professional journals of social work, Federal Probation,
etc., and in books in the field. It is being used in many
institutions which deal with complex behavior problems.

It is used in homes, church, and church related work. To
help readers to have an understanding of the theory, the
author gives a very simple plan which has been used. It
was written up in a social work class at the University of
Michigan School of Social Work.

1. Identify the specific problem behavior. This
   theory emphasizes the now--not the past or
   future. The problem with which the author
   dealt was a problem of temper tantrums of a
   five-year-old boy in day care.

.2. Specify the effects of the situation or environment contributing to the problem. In
   this specific problem two factors seemed to
   be contributing to the problem.

   a. The staff spent considerable time trying,
      during the display of temper, to draw the
      child's attention to toys or other desire-
      able objects. The more they tried the
      more he threw his spells of lying on the
      floor, kicking, and screeming. He "watched"
      for the workers to come to him and respond
      to his behavior. Over a period of several
      "spells" more and more of the staff's time
      was elicited with no change in behavior.

   b. The parents in the home always gave in to
      him when he exhibited the undesirable be-
      havior by giving him attention at his demands.

99

3. Discover the existing behavioral level. This child had spells of throwing temper tantrums at home when his mother did not give in to his demands. This had started at age four. The spells had increased in number and length. They took place at irregular intervals, but as often as he "needed them." When he was admitted to the day care center, a temper tantrum occurred upon entrance to the center each morning--at seven o'clock. There were other exhibitions in the morning and in the afternoon before his mother called for him around five o'clock. He would exhaust himself each time he had a tantrum. The "spells" lasted from five to fifteen minutes. The episodes happened in the building or on the play ground. Sand and dirt made no difference to B. He did not mind getting dirt on his face and in his ears, nose, and mouth. He managed not to get dirt in his eyes.

4. Plan for behavioral change

   a. Assessment of the situation. It was postulated that the staff's attention might actually be reinforcing the temper tantrums intermittently by displaying a tolerant attitude toward them. It was further agreed that coddling the child in the home, at the

time of the episodes, could also be a reinforcer for the undesirable behavior. For
behavioral change to occur, the influence
of environmental variables must be controlled.

b. After determining the diagnosis of the socio-
behavioral problem, the goal of desired behavioral change was agreed upon by the staff
and the mother. There was agreement that
this undesirable behavior could be effected
by differential reinforcement procedures,
whereby response related to desirable behavior would be positively reinforced while
temper tantrums would be extinguished by
withholding any reinforcement or by punishment by disapproval shown by ignoring them.
Staff attention was made dependent upon
appropriate behavior. The parents were en-
listed to cooperate in the behavioral change
technique in the home and in the day care
center. Ordinarily, a specific schedule
would be set up. There was no set schedule
of reinforcement in this case. The concept
of timing or appropriateness was the agreed
upon plan--every time a temper tantrum was
displayed the workers were to walk away
and completely ignore this behavior. Each

time a desirable behavior was exhibited some
reinforcer was to be immediately used. The
differential reinforcements which were varie
and appropriately used were: "a smile," "a
nod of the head," "Good B.," or some favored
food such as "cookies." The schedule or
appropriate time for reinforcement was to be
carefully considered, as well as the amount
and type of reinforcement. Close observation was necessary to notice any response
which might be reinforced. The reinforcement was given immediately when desirable
behavior was performed, lest the child see
no connection between the behavior and the
reinforcer. When B. was playing marbles,
hit the "center man" and laughed with glee,
a staffer "smiled" and said, "Good B."
This change technique was to be continued
daily until the desired behavioral change wa
effected. Reinforcement should be continuou
for ceasing to give reinforcement often
brings rapid decline. The cooperation of
parents and staff made possible a continuous plan at home and in day care. Each time
B. had a temper tantrum, the experimenters
walked away from him, thus punishing him by

turning to other activities or to other children who were behaving appropriately. The planned procedure continued at day care and at home for two months.

5. Consequences of the change operation.

When the change operation was started, B. began to look puzzled. Within a week there was a slight difference in the length of each temper tantrum. The spells became as short as five minutes, especially at the time of entering the center and the one after lunch. Then, for a month there was little change. Toward the end of the month he entered the center with a smile on his face, but would still have a "spell" after his mother left him. By the end of five weeks he was able to enter the center in the morning without displaying the undesirable behavior. He also left off the ill behavior episode right after lunch before "nap time." The inappropriate behavioral demonstrations were continually reduced at the center and at home. The sixth week B. had temper tantrums only on Monday. The length of the time in "temper" was shorter. During the seventh week he had only one "spell" on Monday.

The principle of operant behavior was used by providing the children in day care the

opportunity to exercise the skeletal-muscular
system by using a "climbing tower" and other
play equipment.  The use of these muscles bears
out the theses of the effectiveness of stimulus--
response stressed by some authorities in the
field of operant-conditioning.  The stretching
of the muscles by climbing was provided twice
each day.  The experience on the "climbing tower"
replaced the temper tantrum on Monday of the
eighth week.  These exercises had not effected
change before.  The staff reinforced him with
"smiles," "nods," and expressions such as "great
B."

Occasional relapse into the old behavior was evident through the eighth week in the home.  The
continued opportunities and direct reinforcement by the staff prevented the return of
temper tantrums in the day care center.

This behavioral problem along with many others are
amenable to the socio-behavioral approach.  They can be effected by timely and appropriate positive reinforcements for
desirable behavior, while extinguishing the undesirable behavior by punishing through walking away from and ignoring
the unacceptable behavior.  This simple example demonstrates
one application of behavioral modification techniques to the
alteration of specific behavior.  After two months B. had no

temper tantrums while in the day care center.

This technique may be especially helpful to churches in dealing with problems of tardiness, breaking rules of a game, training in responsibility, "acting-out behavior," anxiety reduction, delinquency, and many others. The illustration given here has shown the application of the following simple principles which may be used by persons with little training:  positive reinforcement (a food), differential reinforcement (smile, verbal expressions, good), extinction (withholding any reinforcement), and punishment (walking away from B. instead of giving in to his demands).

A second proven technique for bringing about behavioral change is providing an opportunity for membership in a club.  The basic needs of belonging and feeling useful are often met through the small club group.  "The warm atmosphere, companionship, acceptance, and understanding help members to understand themselves and others.  This may make it possible for the correction of socially unacceptable behavior, give an impetus to individual achievement, as well as stimulate the assuming of responsibility for one's own personal appearance and actions.  In a Christian setting the club often becomes a channel of divine blessing."[1]

---

[1] Melton, Alpha, Graded Bible Clubs for the Church, Southwestern Baptist Theological Seminary, Box 22277, Fort Worth, Texas, 76122, 1969, p. 2.

## CHAPTER V

## CREATIVE IDEAS FOR INVOLVEMENT

The ideas for church member involvement in this chapter are the result of thought, observation of needs, and suggestions over recent years. Different ethnic groups of students have been asked to express their concern for ministering to others. The ideas are for the purpose of reaching the lost, enlisting those not attending a church, bridging gaps of misunderstanding, or of helping in some area of human need. The overall goal is for the church through member involvement to show love and acceptance of individuals in tangible areas which those being helped understand. When mature Christian love is shown and expressed God uses it to make an impression for good and often to bear fruit unto salvation.

These ideas are briefly stated to serve as guides for interested churches to develop specific plans suited to the needs of the neighborhood people to be served by the church. The groups could meet once each week on a chosen day and time. A trained adult should work with each group. Some of the ideas are spiced with creative acronyms.

106

## Conversational Discovery Fellowship

This idea may be used to develop skill in speaking English or some other language; to understand the Bible as it relates to everyday life or to understanding different religions in the light of God's word; to develop awareness and appreciation of different cultures; to bring about understanding and acceptance of different ethnic groups; to provide friendship for service men, or students away from home or for internationals in our country; to provide a group for the lonely; or to administer therapy for persons with problems such as alcholism, drug addiction, deviant behavior, and mental health.

## Christian Concern Group

This group is an adult or adult and youth group set up to investigate and discuss neighborhood problems and to promote, through community institutions and agencies, the solution to the problems. Some problems which might be dealt with are:

- Americanization of immigrants and the easing of culture shock.

- Promote better education for the disadvantaged by providing neighborhood youth with scholarships for college.

- Appearing before the city council in behalf of the right treatment of those who have no voice to be heard, such as better garbage disposal in slum areas or better street lighting, etc.

107

. Promoting projects of cooperative effort between
  different races.

## PEP -- Pairing Enables Progress

This idea is an expansion of some plans used by
different churches or other resources. It may be corre-
lated with any services existing within the community.

. Pairing boys with no fathers at home with <u>care-
  fully selected</u> men of the church to provide a
  father figure in the early life of the child
  and to plan special things to do together such
  as fishing, hunting, and other interests of
  each boy.

. Pairing a Christian family with a non-Christian
  family and/or a deprived family to become friends
  and be of mutual help to each other--in material,
  psychological, and spiritual matters.

. Pairing a Christian family with children with a
  widow who has children the same age to provide
  friendship, acceptance, and love to meet needs
  and prevent pangs of severe lonliness.

. Pairing mature, trained men with boys and women
  with girls who are pre-delinquents or delinquents
  to help them with their problems and show love,
  concern, and friendship.

. Pairing persons with aged, invalid, or lonely
  persons to visit and do "nice things" with them
  or in case of need for them.

## 3 G's -- Generation-Gap-Get-Together

This group is designed to build understanding and a
closer relationship between teenagers and their parents.
Special open discussions, retreats, trips, films, talent
programs, banquets, cook-outs, and such like have great potential if planned and carried out by the group of families
bound together with purpose.

108

## TAP -- Teen Aiders Program

Since teenagers are continually searching, often searching to find an outlet for self-expression, this idea has great potential of bringing self-actualization to teen-agers, more satisfaction to them and to their families, while at the same time providing services to other persons and agencies. Numberless individually chosen activities are possible through the summer months, such as helping in homes with children when a mother is sick, taking care of children with Christian activities at neighborhood washa-terias, while mothers do the laundry, doing special services for the aging, serving in hospitals, using talents such as music, art, drama, typing, etc., in areas where there is need. The services may be done at the church, at the place of need (washateria), or in some community service agency.

There should be fellowship for reporting on services done, for recognitions, fun, inspiration for meeting what-ever needs the teens have, and for choosing other services in which they are interested in participating.

## Consumer Education and Marketing

This plan may be initiated by a Christian couple or number of couples from the church to reach out to include one or more families who are interested in helping themselves.

The group sets up definite policies of operation, such as
what to buy, when to meet for sharing, and agreement on
paying each week as they share on a non-profit basis. They
may choose a special day to meet in one of the homes to sha
with each other. This can be effective in bringing hope to
hopeless families when Christians care enough to share then
selves and their concern in a constructive way. Food as
well as other items may be purchased with great savings to
the entire group. With Christian witnesses hopeless families can also gain spiritual insight and satisfaction
through Christ and his love.

## Community Living Centers

Churches have great opportunity for becoming involved in helping persons in need to develop their own capa
cities in adjusting or readjusting to life in the "world,"
for children who will later be adopted, or for the aging wh
need special help. The idea here is for homes of church me
bers to be used as half-way houses from a hospital (after
mental or physical sicknesses), detention home for delinquents, to help prepare the individual for more victorious
and abundant living in their own homes or neighborhood.

## CUP -- Community Understanding
Project

This group is to be made up of adults and youth of
whatever ethnic groups live in the neighborhood. The

meetings are held weekly in various homes in the neighborhood or at a church at a convenient time determined by the group. The purpose is to discuss problems of interest and concern of the group for the betterment of individuals within the group, the entire group, or of the community. Discussion leaders may be selected from the group or from the broader community. Each group might have a "chaplain" (one who has had a personal experience with God, lives a Christian life, understands the Scripture, has ability to accept, understand, love and counsel people, and share Christ with those who need him). Each group has a skilled group worker who leads the group in discussions and in setting goals and making plans for trips or projects to better understand the situations as they are and to determine Christian strategies for solving problems. Topics for consideration and visits to be made might include law enforcement agencies, courts, probation departments, jails, city council, and other city organizations; hospitals, clinics and health department, board of education, schools, colleges; public utility companies--powerplant, water, sewerage disposal; fire department; highway department; welfare agencies; convention centers; churches; plus other public and private agencies. It is possible through such cooperative effort for people to become more understanding, accepting, and respectful of each other and more appreciative of the community as they become involved in the work for the good of all people. If

111

the group becomes a large group, sub-groups may be formed
for various functions such as study, implementation of
plans, meeting with various agency personnel for solution
of problems, prayer and Bible study and other groups deemed
essential to meet the needs of persons.

## Drop-In Center

These centers are to be adapted to meet the needs
of ages from teens through the aged.  Churches may use a
room in the church with an outside door decorated or
labeled.  The same room might be used for aged groups during
the day and for youth in the evening.  Mature and dependable
adults need to be present as sponsors and witnesses to wel-
come persons, provide games and equipment, or to meet whatever needs the center is planned to meet.  Different church
groups may be formed such as drama, music, or whatever the
church finds of interest and value in this ministry.  The
room should be attractive and appropriately furnished to provide the right atmosphere.  The center might be very effecti
as a high school student center for certain evenings or afte
school where youth could have a place to go to associate with
other young people in a Christian setting and where adults
care and understand them.

## Entire Church Involvement

I believe that each church should involve every
church member in an outreach of love and concern.  One way

by which this may be done is to divide the church neighborhood into small zones so that not over eight to ten families are in a zone. A mature dedicated Christian couple
would be appointed by the church to be leaders of the group.
The neighborhood group would organize for effective service
by having an appropriate number of subgroup chairmen for
groups such as adult, single adult, teen, pre-teen and
children. One group could meet in one home while another
group met in another home each week. By having the preteens, children, and adults meet together there would be three
groups. Once a month all of the families would meet together for fellowship, prayer, and planning together for
more effective spiritual growth of the families. The members would always be on the lookout for unchurched and un-
saved persons within the zone. The members by becoming
well acquainted with others would become conscious of
bearing one another's burdens. With a well trained couple
as zone leaders many psychological and spiritual needs
might be met. The cooperation with the pastor and other
church staff has the potential of creating a closer knit
Christian fellowship within the entire church membership.
It can also alleviate feelings of neglect, left-outness,
and other very common feelings of members of large congre-
gations where it is impossible for a pastor to visit and
shepherd the large flock.

# RIP -- Retirement Involvement Plan

Retired men and women often feel laid-on-a-shelf because they are not called upon, are not active as they once were, and feel that their wisdom and talents are often not wanted or needed. Some churches are magnificently taking care of this need while others are not. At first a church group of retired people could work up a skill bank by finding out all of the interests, skills, and talents of the retired persons. A file of the skills or talents could be used by the church group in setting goals to use these skills in service to others through the church community. One church used the talents of retired men by buying a church truck which was used by one group to pick up donated toys and furniture to bring to a special place for renovation and distribution. Another group would work with renovation of toys, while another worked with furniture--repairing, painting, reupholstering, etc. The furniture was used to help families in case of emergencies. Retired ladies worked with donated clothing and made quilts and new clothes for families in distress. Some could do telephoning services for the church. Others might give piano lessons for a small sum to community groups who could not afford to pay a regular fee. Those with ways to travel and who are able could feel of service by visiting shut-ins hospitals, or other places where this service is needed.

114

## Conclusion

The ideas for church member involvement and outeach might be easily carried out through existing church rganizations. The goal is that needs be met by a loving, erving, compassionate, forgiving church and that people ome to a saving and living faith in Christ.

People are the church, people represent the church, eople speak by their lives and by their word. What do hey say? These anonymous poems speak to the church:

A little more kindness,
A little less creed;
A little more giving,
A little less greed.

A little more smile,
A little less frown;
A little less kicking a man
When he is down.

A little more "we",
A little less "I";
A little more laugh,
A little less cry.

A little more flowers on the
pathway of life,
And fewer on graves at the
end of life.

***************************

<u>Love</u> has a hem of its garment
that touches the very dust;
It can reach the stains in the streets
and lanes, and because it can, it must.
It dares not rest on the mountains,
it is bound to come to the vale,
For it cannot find its fulness of mind,
till it falls on the lives that fail.

CHAPTER VI

PERSONS HELPED THROUGH COMPASSIONATE
INVOLVEMENT

## From Fear to Hope through Faith

Fear gripped the heart of Mrs. H. She went to an
excellent surgeon for an examination. She had been examined twice before but now she just knew that she had
cancer. The doctor had said that she did not have cancer.
Surgery would certainly fix her up. Her life was miserable. It had become a nightmare. She couldn't sleep. She
was living in mortal fear.

She decided that she had had enough. There had to
be some help. This Christian lady was about 42 years old.
It was evident that she had to have some relief. She was
a victim of her own disbelief. Her mind and heart were
set on the fact that she could not go on living as a
frightened person. Life was too short to fill every day
with worry. One day she was brought to face the issue in
prayer. She called upon the Lord with faith and put her
health and life into the hands of Christ.

When she went back to the doctor he asked if she
had had surgery. She told him no. He replied, "You have

a scar exactly like you have had an operation!" Mrs. H. said, "All I have done is call upon my Lord and put my health and my life in his hands."

## New Life through Love and Care

Mrs. B. was a beautiful young mother with three children. She had to have her teeth extracted. There was no money to buy new teeth. Her husband was a slothful worker and was not good to his family. There was not enough money to provide the bare necessities for the family. Mrs. B. was folding up within herself. A loving, compassionate Christian in a great church felt for and with her. She presented a challenge to Mrs. B. and to the youth in a church. They started saving money to buy her some teeth. The church related agency started saving money.

A few weeks passed and there was enough money for the expense of an impression and having dentures made. The day came for making the impression. Then, waiting to get the new teeth. This was a happy day. The loving, caring, and sharing paid off. Every person who was involved in this effort was blessed. Mrs. B. became more beautiful and outgoing with her new possession. The teeth were beautiful. She became more loving and began reaching out to others until she became a leader and dependable worker in another church. She took on new life and is still serving today. Love and compassionate action made the difference.

## From Desire for Death to Fuller Life

S. was almost a teenager.  She had never walked.
She slid on the floor with crippled legs bent under her.
She thought she would never walk.  Her family had no hope
for she was born a cripple.  Day-by-day the routine of
nothingness made her life miserable.  She in turn made
others unhappy.

A church became interested in her.  The pastor knew
how to cooperate in using the community resources for the
good of people.  S. was impatient, dissatisfied, and hopeless.  She was continually frustrated, giving up, and not
caring.

S. wanted to be like other girls.  She wanted to
walk, run, and play.  She wanted to be free.  She was
physically crippled.  There was danger of her also becoming a cripple mentally.  She had a good mind and a beautiful, winsome personality, but she was blighted with self-
pity and fear.

One day she realized that she was not alone.  Help
and understanding were coming from above and through the
small church.  A civic agency had become interested also.
A hospital was contacted.  Compassionate concern of church,
community, and outside agencies in combined Christian social
action brought hope to this hopeless girl.  Surgery straight-
ened the crooked little legs.  After weeks in the hospital

118

. came home.

Today she lives and walks erect. She has a husband
and several children. She drives the family car and goes
where she wants to. It took cooperative effort to make
his possible. Her physical well-being was out of her hands.
he and her family trusted those who cared and through the
xperiences S. learned to trust God.

## An Aged Man's First Rocking Chair

Mr. M. was an aged man with a young wife and six
hildren. The tiny house was made of discarded roofing,
umber, and whatever could be picked up without cost. There
as one room and a kitchen. The floor was the earth on
hich the house was built. There were two beds and no chairs
n the home.

Mr. M. became very sick. A young social work student
ecame interested in the family. Community agencies were
ontacted. Food, medicine, and bare necessities were prov-
ded. Mr. M. could not rest lying down, but he had no chair
o sit in.

A white wicker rocking chair was taken to the home.
r. M. and the family responded like most families would act
ver a new car. He sat, rested, and rocked for five hours
n the chair. When he went back to bed the children fussed
ver who would sit in the chair.

The family was so thrilled because they had found
rue friends who really cared about them - friends who

"loveth at all times" (Prov. 17:17).  As they talked and
found out that the friends loved because Christ had loved
them, they began to study the Bible.  They believed that
the Bible was God's Word.  Before many weeks had passed
Mr. M. and several children trusted Jesus as their Saviour

Many friends of this family who remember this case
story have said, "When we get to heaven and see the man
who enjoyed his first rocking chair, we want to ask him if
the old chair had anything to do with his decision for
Christ."  Was it the chair or the love which constrained
the giving of the chair which influenced the change?

## Courage Tested in Poverty

M. was aware that society is geared toward achieve
ment and "middleclassness."  To be honest with herself and
society, she felt that she must take courage to own up to
being poor.  She worked hard to dress well.  Her friends
"away from her home" might have thought from her appearanc
that she was a little rich girl.  She kept on with her goo
and acceptable appearance, but was honest that often at hon
there was not enough food and that one family member ate
with a spoon while another ate with a fork for there was n
enough "silver" to go around.  Since poverty is often a
state of mind or spirit, M. disarmed the sharp sting from
poverty with her honesty and courage.

120

## Courage Tested in Prejudice

A deacon's wife came to her pastor and said, "Please
pray for me, I surely have prejudice in my heart." Her
church was changing from a one ethnic group membership to
one of many groups. This honesty was half the battle won
in her heart. She did not play being free in accepting
everyone, but faced up to her own inadequacy. Because of
this courage and her desire to change, God changed her
heart.

## Courage to Laugh Through Tears

K. was a beautiful teenage girl who was an expect-
ant mother before marriage. She faced the problem with
great courage while she was in a home for unwed mothers.
Church groups did special things with and for the group
of which she was a part. She mixed well with the groups
and participated in every activity. Love and acceptance
shortened the time away from home. The experiences, openness, and awareness, brought about greater knowledge of herself and of others. Because of her ability to cope with
this situation, she was likewise coping with a new life
back home. Christian women helped to make a difference
in her managing her problem. The church group also developed, became aware of their weaknesses, and learned not
to pass judgment.

# BIBLIOGRAPHY

Beall, Jewel Chancy. Baptist Centers Reaching a Contemporary World. Division of Missions, Home Mission Board. Atlanta, Georgia: Southern Baptist Convention, 1964.

Konopka, Gisela. Social Group Work: A Helping Process. Englewood Cliffs, N. Y.: Prentice Hall, Inc., 1963.

Melton, Alpha. Graded Bible Clubs for the Church. Fort Worth: Southwestern Baptist Theological Seminary, Box 22277, 1969.

Nelson, Marion H., M.D. Why Christians Crack Up. Chicago: Moody Press, n.d.

Vinter, Robert D. Readings in Group Work Practice. Ann Arbor, Michigan: Campus Publishers, 1968.

Wirt, Sherwood Eliot. The Social Conscience of the Evangelical. New York: Harper and Row, 1968.

Younger, George D. The Church and Urban Renewal. New York: J. B. Lippincott Company, 1965.